Yellow onion skins with alum mordant on wool

Alkanet roots with no mordant on wool

Elderberries with chrome mordant on wool

Indigo with alum mordant on wool (Meth

Indigo with alum mordant on sisal (Method No. 1)

Indigo with alum mordant on cotton (Method No. 1)

Indigo with alum mordant on wool (Method No. 2)

Logwood with no mordant on wool

Logwood with copperas mordant on wool

Annatto with alum mordant on wool

Bloodroot with no mordant on wool

Bloodroot with alum mordant on wool

Gum catechu, no mordant on wool

Henna with tin mordant on wool

Henna with tin mordant on mohair

Lily of the valley with chrome mordant on wool

Madder and sedge with alum mordant on wool

Pokeweed berries with chrome mordant on wool

Burley tobacco with blue vitriol mordant on wool

Cocklebur with copperas mordant on wool

Goldenrod blossoms with copperas mordant on wool

Goldenrod blossoms, indigo, alum mordant on wool

Goldenrod plant, copperas mordant on wool

Gum catechu, blue vitriol mordant on wool No. 1

Alma Lesch

VEGETABLE DYEING

151 COLOR RECIPES FOR DYEING YARNS AND FABRICS WITH NATURAL MATERIALS

WATSON-GUPTILL PUBLICATIONS/NEW YORK

Dedicated to the memory of Nelle Peterson

Copyright 1970 by Watson-Guptill Publications,
a division of Billboard Publications, New York.

All rights reserved.

Manufactured in the U.S.A.

No portion of the contents of this book
may be reproduced or used in any form or by
any means without the written permission of
the publishers.

International Standard Book Number: 0-8230-5600-7

Library of Congress Catalog Card Number: 70-87323

Preface

The purpose of this book is to provide an informative guide for those who wish to dye their own fibers with natural substances.

The general information gives instructions for making dyes from the various types of natural substances and instructions for dyeing natural fibers with them. The recipes provide instructions for dyeing specific fibers with specific substances.

I have attempted to relate this information to the tradition of vegetable dyeing by eliminating many chemical and botanical terms. It is a practical guide rather than an exhaustive and technical one.

I am indebted to the American Crafts Council, especially Lois Moran, Director of Education and Research; Dr. J. J. Oppenheimer, former Dean of Arts and Sciences and former Chairman of the Education Department, University of Louisville; Martha Christensen, Supervisor of Art for the Louisville Public Schools; and to present and former students at the Louisville School of Art for their encouragement and assistance while this work was being completed.

Alma Lesch
Shepherdsville, Kentucky
November 1969

Contents

I. General Information

Vegetable dyeing is a craft which has existed since the earliest times, and it has a celebrated history. The distinctive color quality that it creates can be recognized almost immediately. The present generation of textile craftsmen is extremely sensitive to color, and perhaps this is the main reason for the recent interest in this particular craft.

This book is designed to provide some practical information on vegetable dyeing. The information is divided into three parts: general information, specific information, and reference material.

The general information provides a background to the general practices in the preparation and performance of activities relating to dye substances, fibers, and dyes.

The recipes give specific information for making dyes in primary and secondary color ranges, and ranges of browns and blacks. These sample recipes use yarns, in a variety of fibers, in combinations with dye substances and mordants. They show the properties of the mordants and their effect on color and fiber.

It is important to understand that there is a considerable amount of risk in vegetable dyeing because of the variables involved. Plants grown in different geographical areas which have their own particular seasonal and climatic conditions, may produce different shades, and sometimes different colors, from the plants used to make the dyes in these recipes. Commercially supplied dyestuffs also produce color variances for the same reasons. Even with specific directions the results are often unpredictable.

The reference material lists sources of supply for chemicals, fibers, and dye substances, which may not be easily available. The charts provide a quick informational guide in the areas of color and dye substances. The bibliography lists books which supply information on additional areas of vegetable dyeing, such as plant identification, poisonous plants, the history of dyestuffs, and other methods of dyeing.

The material in this book should be treated as a point of departure for making vegetable dyes, and as an indication of how they can be used to one's own advantage.

EQUIPMENT AND WORK SPACE

Vegetable dyeing can be done in any area—a kitchen, laboratory, workshop, or school room—as long as the work space has ventilation, light, water, heat, storage space, counters or tables, and stools for physical comfort. The picturesque kettle, hanging in outdoor areas from a tripod with a wood fire under it, makes a delightful environment but it both prolongs the time requirements for the processes and is only possible in certain seasons. It is easier to do vegetable dying indoors.

Also, if the equipment for the job is assembled and grouped according to the activity and progression of the jobs, the work will be easier and quicker. Suggested equipment for the various vegetable dyeing activities is as follows:

For skeining:

Yarn winder or improvised apparatus
Scissors
String

For collecting dye materials:

Scissors
Hand pruners—short one and long handled one
Leather gloves
Sharp knives—long blade one and short blade one
Axe
Small hand saw
Paper bags—one-sixth of a barrel size
Cardboard boxes
Labels
Insect repellent—for collector

For storing dye materials:

Access to refrigeration
Access to freezer
Dry, ventilated space, such as attic, garage, shed, or extra room, for storing dry materials
One gallon buckets, plastic or glass jugs, and jars
Cardboard boxes
Paper and cloth bags
Labels
Freezer bags

For storing and mixing chemicals:

Glass bottles with screw on glass tops for sulfuric acid and other dangerous chemicals. Let the number and size fit the need.
Airtight glass containers
Rubber gloves
Glass rods for stirring
Dowels for mixing
Glass funnel or flask
Glass measures—pint, quart, and gallon
Set of kitchen measuring spoons
One ounce shot glass
Rags
(Store chemicals in manufacturer's container if possible)

For storing dye baths:

Covered glass or plastic jars or jugs
Access to freezer

For scouring:

Two or three, two or three gallon enamel dish pans
Two or three, one gallon enamel pans
Three or four, twenty quart size enamel home canners with covers
Dowels and sticks for stirring and lifting yarns
Rags and towels

For mordanting:

Two or three, two or three gallon enamel dish pans
Two or three, one gallon enamel pans
Three or four, twenty quart size, enamel home canners with covers
Glass bowls, quart and gallon sizes
Glass measures, pint, quart, and gallon sizes
Dowels, glass rods, sticks
Scales that will weigh ounces and pounds
Apothecary or metric scale (useful but not essential)
Mortar and pestle (useful but not essential)
Rags and towels
Set of kitchen measuring spoons

For making dye baths:

Two or three, two or three gallon enamel dish pans
Two or three, one gallon enamel pans
Three or four, twenty quart size, enamel home canners with covers
Glass or plastic one gallon measures
Enamel food strainer or cheesecloth
Five pound size, cotton bags
Dowels and sticks
Rags
Set of kitchen measuring spoons
Glass measures, pint and quart sizes

For dyeing:

Two or three, two or three gallon enamel dish pans
Two or three, one gallon enamel pans
Three or four, twenty quart size enamel home canners with covers
Rags and towels
Dowels and sticks
Rubber gloves
Gallon measures

This equipment can serve more than one function—the same pans and home canners can be used for scouring, mordanting, and dyeing. It should be assembled to fit the need and in relation to the number of people working at the same time.

DOCUMENTING

Documenting and keeping records are very important in vegetable dyeing.

Chemicals should be labeled and stored in the proper kind of container in a safe, dry place, preferably one that is locked. Special caution should be taken with sulfuric acid and other dangerous chemicals.

The purchased dye materials, such as powders, berries and barks, should be labeled and stored in the proper kind of container in a dry place.

The dye materials one collects for oneself should be labeled and stored according to the nature of the materials.

Dyed yarns should be tagged and the information pertaining to the particular dyed yarn should be listed on the tag. This will prevent future mistakes, it avoids the making of duplicates, and helps in experimenting with additional dyes and mordants. Shades of color are often too close to distinguish by memory. Documented dyed yarns are often needed to level a batch of yarns from the same dye material and mordant, dyed at different times, to make them into one shade.

Information on the tag attached to the dyed yarns should include:

Dye material

Season of collection or purchase

Mordant

If dye bath is used more than once, note number of times

Kind of fiber

Date yarn was dyed

A tag cut from brown paper, looped over and taped to one of the strings tied around the skeins of yarns, could read like this:

Sedge

Collected in summer

Chrome mordant

Second dye bath

Wool fibers

Dyed—August, 1969

COLLECTING DYE MATERIALS

The often used term *vegetable dye* could be misleading, and the term *natural dye* is actually more correct. Some of the natural materials which make dyes are not vegetable matter. Cochineal, for instance, comes from an insect; some clays make dyes, and there are other exceptions. Most of the traditional dye materials—such as indigo, cochineal, barks of trees not native to this country, madder in quantity, etc.—must be purchased from commercial suppliers.

Natural materials differ according to climate conditions and geographical regions and the vegetable dyer should collect the dye materials in any area for the dyer to obtain a working assortment of vegetable dye colors, and his own assortment can be supplemented from commerical suppliers.

The time of the year when the material is collected, and the growing conditions of the season, determine the quality of color that most vegetable materials contain. Berries, blossoms, and most above the ground plant parts must have a lot of hot sunshine to produce strong dye colors. Hot and dry, but not too dry, weather produces the best colors. Material should generally be cut as late in the season as possible and when it is in peak growth condition. Vegetable dyers have good years and bad for collecting dye materials.

The large paper bags, one sixth of a barrel size, are good containers to use when collecting materials. One full bag, fairly tightly packed, will make the four gallons of cut up materials called for in many of these recipes and will dye a minimum of one pound of yarns.

To collect barks and roots: Barks and roots should be collected in late winter or spring, when the sap is up. Theoretically, they contain more color substance at this time. It is foolish to destroy a tree to get bark for a dye bath, but a small amount of bark can be removed from the trunk of a tree without killing it. It is a good idea to utilize the barks and roots from trees that have to be removed.

When entire roots of a plant are dug, it will, of course, die. However, small sections of roots or root systems can be removed without permanent injury to the plants and trees.

Commercial suppliers often do a better job of collecting and supplying barks and roots than the do-it-yourself collector.

To collect berries and fleshy fruits: As a general rule, only the dark color berries and fleshy fruits make dyes and not all of them. This group of materials should be picked when they are completely ripe.

To collect blossoms: Blossoms for vegetable dye purposes can be cut when the flower first reaches full bloom. Not all blossoms make dyes.

To collect clays: Clays can be collected at any time of the year. Collect generous amounts to allow for loss caused by drying and by removal of foreign matter.

To collect grasses, leaves, stalks, stems, twigs, and vines: Collect this group of materials as late in the season as the plant part is still in good physical condition. These need a season's weather to make dye substances. Twigs and vines should usually have one to two years growth. Sprouts and seedlings do not make good dyes; it is better to cut two to three feet lengths from branches. Some grasses are good sources of dye if they are collected between late spring and the first frost.

To collect nut hulls and shells: It is usually the hull or shell of the nut that yields the dye. These should be collected only when the nuts are mature, usually after they have fallen to the ground, and sometimes after frost. It is not advisable to make dyes from nut hulls or shells after they have been on the ground through a winter's weather. The hulls and shells of nuts can be broken off by hand, or tapped with another object to loosen the hull.

Black walnuts, for instance, make stronger dyes if they are used when they appear green with brown spots on them.

It is important to understand that plants are known by different names in different locations. If there is any difficulty in making identifications of vegetable materials, a book on horticulture should be consulted.

PRESERVING DYE MATERIALS

The dye materials which have been purchased from commercial suppliers should be labeled and stored in a dry place. Since they are expensive, it is worth storing them carefully.

Dye materials collected for oneself can be preserved by freezing, or by drying them in a very slow oven or in the air. Some color may be lost from the dehydration or drying, but little or no color is lost from freezing.

To preserve barks and roots: It is preferable to dry barks and roots in the air because of the slower drying process, and the possibility of causing a fire by oven drying. To do this, place the barks and roots one layer deep in a dry, well ventilated space and allow them to remain there until completely dry. If they are turned over or their arrangement is shifted, it speeds up the drying.

When they are dry, label them, place them in porous containers, such as paper or cloth bags, and store in a dry place. Large roots and chunks of barks can be labeled, placed in a pile, and stored out of the weather.

Barks and roots should be soaked from twenty-four to seventy-two hours before they are used for dye baths; the length of time needed for soaking will, of course, depend on the size of the material.

To preserve berries and fleshy fruits: Some of the berries and fleshy fruits can be dried, but often in the drying process there is either some loss of color, or an actual change in color. For example, pokeweed berries turn brown when dried, and make dye bath colors other than red.

To dry berries and fleshy fruits, place them in a dry, well ventilated space, one layer deep, and allow them to dry naturally in the air. They should be turned over at least once daily. After they are dry, label them, place them in porous containers, such as paper or cloth bags, and store them in a dry place.

It is, on the other hand, possible to freeze berries and fleshy fruits with little or no loss of color. Just measure them, place the unwashed berries or fruits in plastic freezer bags, label each one and store the bags immediately in a food freezer. It will not be necessary to thaw these materials before using them. To make the dye bath, cover the measured amount of berries or fruits with the right amount of water, and boil gently until the color is removed.

To preserve blossoms: There are some blossoms which cannot be preserved, such as goldenrod and dandelion, and these must be used fresh. However, others can be dried in the air, or in a very slow oven.

To dry blossoms in the air, just spread them one layer deep in a dry, well ventilated space and allow them to remain there until dry. Turning or shifting their positions, especially those of the large blossom heads, tends to speed up the process. If there are large flowers among them, their petals can be picked off and dried by themselves. Blossoms sometimes lose some color from drying.

If the slow oven process is going to be used to dry the blossom, the cooking stove oven should be set on the lowest warm temperature. Then the blossoms should be placed in a large metal container and allowed to remain there until dry. The time it will take depends on the size of the blossoms. It is a good idea to stir or move the blossoms often, and to leave the oven door open to help maintain a very low temperature. When the blossoms are dry, label, place them in porous containers, such as paper or cloth bags, and store in a dry place.

Do not freeze blossoms.

To preserve clays: Clays should be allowed to dry naturally. Then label them and store in a dry place. If the clays are dried in a kiln or oven it will not affect the color, but this is unnecessary. Dry clays are easier to pulverize and separate from foreign matter than wet clays.

To preserve grasses, leaves, stalks, stems, twigs, and vines: This group of materials should not be frozen. They should be preserved by air drying, although this method often causes the loss of some color content.

Place the materials one layer deep in a dry, well ventilated space and allow them to dry naturally from air. Again, turning or shifting their positions will speed up the drying process. When the material is dry, place small pieces in porous containers, such as paper or cloth bags, then label and store them in a dry place. The grasses, stalks, and vines can be tied in bunches, labeled, and hung from ceilings, rafters, or walls. It is not a good idea to attempt to dry this group of materials in an oven because of the danger from fire.

This group of materials should be soaked before they are made into a dye bath. Of course, the length of the soaking time will depend on the size of materials.

To preserve nut hulls and shells: The hulls and shells of nuts can be preserved on or off the nut. In this case, natural air drying is preferable to oven drying. To preserve the nuts, hulls, or shells, just spread them one layer deep in a dry, well ventilated space and allow them to remain there until dry. When they are dry, place them in porous containers, label, and store in a dry place. The hulls and shells can be broken off the nuts any time after being dried. Some color is always lost from dehydration.

The dried hulls and shells should be soaked for about twenty-four hours before using them for a dye bath.

PRESERVING DYE BATHS

Vegetable dye baths will spoil, ferment, or mold at room temperature within two or three days, unless precautions are taken to preserve them. If they are to remain fresh enough to use for several days, they must be stored in a cool place or refrigerated. Spoiled vegetable baths are often unfit for use; they will change color or give off toxic fumes when heated.

However, some of the dye baths can be used after they have molded; these retain their original color and the mold can be simply dipped off. Others that have changed colors can be used if desired. Still others should not be used at all. The dyer will learn from experience when and whether to use dye baths that are not freshly made. For example, when the pokeweed berry ferments, the dye bath turns brown and dyes brown, giving off a repugnant odor and fumes which may be toxic to sensitive individuals. This is why all vegetable dyeing and mordanting should be done in a well ventilated space.

To preserve dye baths by freezing: Dye baths can be preserved almost indefinitely by freezing. Plastic or glass containers should be filled about three fourths full with the dye bath and placed in the freezer. Leave the top off until the liquid is frozen, and then cover it. The frozen dye bath will remain fresh with little loss of color. If thawed it will be ready for use.

To preserve dye baths with sodium benzoate: Sodium benzoate is commonly used as a preservative and it also preserves vegetable dye baths. It can be purchased or ordered from drug stores. Technically, sodium benzoate is used in the amount of one tenth of one percent of volume measure, but one teaspoon per gallon of dye bath is satisfactory. The sodium benzoate powder should be added to the hot liquid and sealed in airtight containers. It will remain fresh for months with little or no loss of color. Vegetable dye baths should never be stored in metal containers.

WATER

Soft water is best for all of the processes of vegetable dyeing, but it is not absolutely necessary. The colors may not be as bright and clear unless soft water is used. Rain water is naturally soft, and it should be used if it is available.

However, since most dyers are not fortunate enough to have a supply of rain water, they must rely on water from central water supply systems. This water is usually hard, because it contains dissolved mineral salts. The water department can supply information on the degree of hardness of any particular supply and well water samples can be sent to city and state laboratories for analysis.

There are other ways in which water can be softened. The most practical solution to water hardness is to use a packaged water softener that is sold in grocery stores.

Alternatively, the dyer can make his own fairly efficient water softener by dissolving one pound of sal soda, known as washing soda, in one quart of boiling water. Stir this until it is completely dissolved. If the water is moderately hard, add two tablespoons of the solution for each gallon of water. A water softener made at home in this way can be bottled and kept almost indefinitely.

Since water temperatures are important to natural fibers, it is wise to know something about them. Lukewarm water temperatures range from 95° to 105°F.; temperatures over 145° are considered hot; simmering temperatures range from about 180° to 210°; and water boils at 212°.

FIBERS

Because of their affinity for vegetable dyes, only the fibers of animal and vegetable origin are used in these vegetable dye recipes, and the fibers are in the form of yarns.

Usually, the form of the fibers is a yarn, since yarns are basic to textiles. However, fabrics and fleeces can be dyed by using the same recipes—they apply to one pound quantities of dry fibers in any form. Yarns, fabrics, and scoured fleeces should always be weighed when they are dry. Often fabrics will dye to lighter shades of color than yarns, and fleeces generally dye to darker tones. It is important to note that the fiber content prevents any two kinds of fibers from appearing to be the same dye lot, even though they were dyed in the same dye bath at the same time.

The common fibers that originate on animals are wool and silk. Those that have a vegetable origin are cotton, grasses and raffia, jute, linen, and sisal. In every case, it is the natural unbleached fibers that give the best results. Although bleached fibers can be used, some of the resiliency has already been destroyed. Any fibers which have had the color stripped from them are not recommended even though, economically, it may be necessary to use them on rare occasions.

There are specific instructions in this book for scouring, mordanting, and dyeing each of the yarn fibers. As far as fabrics, fleeces, and grasses are concerned, the process is much the same as that for yarns, unless specifically mentioned.

MAKING SKEINS OF YARNS

The material in this book is primarily concerned with fibers after they have been spun into yarns. These yarns, either the hand spun or purchased ones, must be made into skeins or hanks for convenience in handling during the processes involved with vegetable dyeing.

The yarns can easily be wound into skeins, and four ounce size skeins make for comfortable handling. A yarn winder can be used if one is available; if it is not, primitive devices can be substituted. For example, skeins can be made by wrapping the yarn around the legs of a stool or a chair, turned upside down. Or, long nails or spikes can be driven into surfaces about 18" to 24" apart and the yarns wound around them. Yarn can be wound around the backs of two straight back chairs placed back to back. Another way is to bend your arm and wind yarn around the hand and elbow. Four ounce skeins are convenient to handle.

After skeins are made, strings should be tied loosely around them in three or four places while they are in the form of an oval or circle. This will prevent tangling when several skeins are placed in the same container.

SCOURING FIBERS

Vegetable dyeing is a process undertaken in three steps: scouring, mordanting, and dyeing. All fibers should be scoured before they are mordanted, and the best results are obtained by using fibers in their natural state. If bleached yarns are used, the length of the time involved in scouring should be about half of the time required for unbleached ones. The water level should be maintained at a height that completely covers the yarns. It is extremely risky to leave the yarns in solutions longer than the prescribed time, since strong acid and alkaline solutions may injure or destroy their resiliency. On the whole, yarns may be left in plain water for a day or two. And, it never hurts to cover the container when scouring, mordanting, and dyeing. This will also help to control steam and odor in the working area. A clothes dryer should not be used in vegetable dyeing; instead, allow the yarns to dry outside in the shade, away from direct sunlight, or inside, at room temperature.

Most wet fibers can be rolled in towels and kept for several days at room temperature, or refrigerated and kept for two weeks, without injury to the fibers. In fact, keeping fibers wet for a few days often increases their affinity for the next process. If wool fibers are refrigerated, they should be allowed to warm to room temperature before beginning the next step; never freeze wool.

The twenty quart size home canner is a good container to use when scouring, mordanting, or dyeing. Of course, the size of the yarns will essentially determine the amount of water needed for each process—a pound of tightly twisted, small size, silk fibers requires less water than a pound of cotton chenille. It is quite possible to scour more than one pound of yarns at the same time, in the same container, if solution requirements are increased accordingly. Basically, the size of the yarn and the tightness of its twist will dictate the length of time requirements for the processes. Several ply, tightly twisted yarns, such as ropes, require a longer time than loosely spun, single ply yarns. Liquids should be squeezed or shaken from animal fibers and most vegetable fibers can withstand twisting and wringing. Any form of mild soap may be used for scouring, but cold water soaps should not be used.

General instructions for scouring are as follows. The scouring bath should be prepared by using a generous amount of warm water for the bulk of yarn, adding water softener, if needed, until water is slick, and adding soap until suds are formed by stirring. Then the yarn should be immersed in the scouring bath and simmered or boiled from twenty minutes to one hour, depending on the kind of fiber and whether it is natural or bleached. Finally, cool the yarn, rinse it until all the soap is removed, and remove the water and mordant immediately or let it dry naturally.

ANIMAL FIBERS: The natural oils in animal fibers melt at lower temperatures than the oils in vegetable fibers, and because of this animal fibers should be kept below boiling point, while most vegetable fibers can be boiled. It is never a good idea to subject wool to quick temperature changes; this will cause matting and felting. Wool fibers that are very dirty and oily may have to be scoured more than one time before they are clean. Even more than wool, silk fibers require delicate handling. The timing of the processes, and the additives for solutions, should be less for silk than for wool.

To scour silk yarns: About two gallons of warm water should be used for one pound of dry silk yarns. Water softener can be added, if needed, until water is slick. To scour the yarns, add soap until mild suds are formed by stirring, then immerse them in the liquid and simmer for thirty minutes. Finally, cool the yarns and rinse until soap is removed. Mordant immediately or dry at room temperature.

To scour wool fibers: Two to three gallons of water should be allowed for scouring one pound of dry wool fibers. Again, add water softener, if needed, until water is slick and add soap until mild suds are formed by stirring. Then immerse the wool fibers and simmer for about forty-five minutes. Mohair and other delicate wools should be simmered for about fifteen minutes. If bleached wools are used, simmer them about twenty to thirty minutes. When the fibers have simmered for the appropriate time, cool and rinse until all the soap is removed. Mordant, dry at room temperature, or roll in towels.

If any of the fibers are dried after scouring, they should be soaked in warm water until they are thoroughly wet before mordanting them.

VEGETABLE FIBERS: Vegetable fibers can withstand boiling and quick temperature changes without injury; they can be twisted to remove water from them. However, they normally have less afinity for vegetable dyes than animal fibers, and often do not dye as well or as dark in color.

To scour cotton fibers: Up to two or three gallons of hot water should be used. Add water softener, if needed, until water is slick. Add enough soap to make rich suds by stirring. An additional one half cup of sal soda should be added in this case. Then the cotton fibers should be immersed and boiled for one to two hours, depending on the size and tightness of the twist in the plys of yarns. After boiling, cool the fibers; rinse until soap is removed; remove water; mordant or dry.

To scour jute fibers: The natural jute ropes and strings found in hardware and farm supply stores are darker in color than most other natural fibers. Naturally, this influences the choice of colors for dyeing. The best idea is to obtain bleached or natural jute from yarn suppliers because this will dye to almost any color.

To prepare the scouring bath for one pound of dry jute fibers, run two or three gallons of hot water into enamel container; add water softener, if needed, until water is slick; add soap until rich suds are formed by stirring. An additional half a cup of sal soda should be added, and stirred until dissolved. The jute fibers should then be immersed in the scouring bath, and the hardware variety of jute must be boiled for two hours. Weaving and bleached jute should be boiled for one hour. Cool the jute; rinse until soap is removed; remove water; mordant or dry.

To scour linen: In general, linen fibers are difficult to dye with vegetable dyes. Handkerchief weight linen fabric and soft twist few ply linen yarns will dye fair to good, but heavy linen fabric and linen rug warps are very difficult to dye.

To scour linen, heat about three gallons of water until hot; add water softener, if needed, until water is slick; add enough soap to make rich suds by stirring; also add an additional one half cup of sal soda. Then immerse the fibers in the scouring bath and boil one to two hours, depending on the type of linen fibers. Cool; rinse until soap is removed; remove water; dry or mordant.

To scour raffia and grasses: Special care should be taken in the handling of raffia and grasses because harsh treatment, such as twisting, or the use of chemicals, may destroy them. Usually it's only necessary to soak them in mild soapy water until they are soft, and to rinse them and place them on towels or other absorbent surface to dry. The mordant should be included in the dye bath to eliminate one of the handling processes.

To scour sisal: The sisal ropes and twines found in hardware, farm, and fishing supply stores dye well with dark colors. Sisal bags can be dyed and the yarns from the bags can be pulled out and dyed.

To about three gallons of hot water, add water softener, if needed, until water is slick; add soap until rich suds are formed; add an additional half a cup of sal soda. This should be stirred until the sal soda is completely dissolved. Then, immerse sisal fibers in the scouring bath and boil for one to two hours, depending on the size of the yarns. Cool the fibers; rinse until soap is removed; remove water; mordant or dry.

STRIPPING

Although stripping the color from yarns so they can be used again is not a recommended process, there may be times when it is economically necessary. Unfortunately, stripped yarns often lose their natural resiliency and become lifeless. This is due to the chemicals and the number of processes involved. When aniline dyed yarns are stripped, it means that they have already been bleached and dyed at least one time; vegetable dyed yarns have been scoured, mordanted, and dyed. Stripping the original color and mordanting and dyeing a second time is extremely hard on any fiber content.

Further, stripping does not bring the yarns back to their original natural color. Some of the dyed color is often still left in the yarns; this should always be taken into consideration when choosing the vegetable dye color. Vegetable dyed colors and shades used on stripped yarns are more unpredictable than those used on new fibers.

Perhaps the least harmful stripping method for natural fibers is that of simmering them in a mild soap solution for about thirty minutes and then rinsing them. A new soap solution should be made for each repetition of this process and it should be repeated until as much color as will come out has been removed. After the final rinsing no scouring is needed. The next steps are mordanting and dyeing with vegetable dyes.

The same method can be used for fabrics and fleeces.

MORDANTING OF FIBERS

Mordanting is very important to successful vegetable dyeing and must be done with care. Theoretically, a mordant is any substance which will combine with a dye substance to form a permanent color. However, this is not always true with vegetable dyed fabrics and yarns—some of them may fade even when every precaution is taken. The mordants and Glauber's salts in the recipes of this book are used as aids in making the color fast; without the use of mordants and salts most colors soon wash out or fade because of various environmental conditions.

Often mordants are metallic salts which produce color ranges peculiar to the particular kind of metal from which the salt is made. Tin makes bright colors; copperas darkens colors and gives them greenish, purple, and black tones; chrome makes shades of blue, brasses, golds, and rusts; blue vitriol makes greenish tones. Especially rewarding and unusual results can be achieved by mixing mordants.

Mordants are manufactured in more than one quality. The commercial grade is inexpensive and is quite satisfactory for use in vegetable dyeing. The more refined quality, prepared for pharmaceuticals, can be used, but this is unnecessary and expensive. Remember to handle all chemicals with caution; store them according to the manufacturer's directions, preferably in locked cabinets.

Different amounts of mordants produce different results. For example, in some dyes a small amount of copperas will turn the dye purple, while a larger amount will make it black. However, too much of any mordant will injure the fibers.

To make a mordant solution, three gallons of water is usually enough. The mordants may be mixed with water to form percentage solutions, or they can be measured by the spoonful or ounce. Whichever method of measurement is used, identical repetition of the dye lots cannot be produced. It is possible, however, to use mordant solutions more than one time if half of the original amount of mordant is added for each additional use. Also, different fibers can be mordanted together if the time requirements are the same or, for example, wool can be mordanted with vegetable fibers, removed at the end of one hour and the vegetable fibers left in the mordant for a longer time.

There are probably several methods for mordanting. Three successful ones are:

1. To mordant before the yarns are dyed.
2. To mordant while the yarns are dyeing.
3. To mordant before and after the yarns are dyed.

There are advantages to each method. When the yarns are mordanted before they are dyed, the colors are clearer and there is more control over the mordanting results. However, it is quicker to mordant while the yarns are dyeing, and this eliminates one handling process. And, if the yarns are mordanted before, and after, they are dyed, it can make the colors faster, make brighter and stronger colors, and change the color. In the third method, the yarns can be mordanted with one mordant before dyeing, and another after dyeing. Usually the second mordant should be only half of the amount that would be used in mordanting before dyeing. This amount will not change the basic color, it will only change the tone. A yellow may be made into a different yellow tone by mordanting it with alum before dyeing to produce a green tone, by dyeing, and finally, by mordanting again with a half amount of copperas or blue vitriol. The basic color would be changed if a full amount of mordant is used for the second mordanting, so be careful to use the right amount.

To mordant before the yarns are dyed: For one pound of dry yarns, put three gallons of warm water in a five gallon enamel container, add mordant, and stir until completely dissolved. Wet scoured yarns should then be added. Animal fibers should be allowed to simmer for one hour and vegetable fibers boiled for two hours. After this, cool and rinse the yarns, dye or dry them.

To mordant while the yarns are dyeing: The mordant should be added to the warm dye bath and stirred until completely dissolved. The wet, scoured yarns can then be added and they should simmer or boil for thirty minutes. Then dissolve four tablespoons of tartaric acid and half a cup of Glauber's salts in one pint of hot water and add this mixture to the liquid. Simmer another thirty minutes, and cool the yarns in the liquid. The yarns must then be rinsed in warm water until the rinse is clear. After this, remove water from the yarns and hang them in the shade to dry.

To mordant before and after yarns are dyed: Put three gallons of warm water in a five gallon enamel container, add mordant and stir until it is completely dissolved. Then add wet, scoured yarns and simmer or boil them for one hour, depending on whether they are animal or vegetable fiber yarns. Cool the yarns; rinse; and dye.

If the second mordanting is only intended to produce color fastness, put dyed yarns back in the original mordant and simmer them for about thirty minutes. On the other hand, if the second mordant is intended to change the color, add half the normal amount of mordant to fresh water, dissolve the mordant, add the dyed yarns and simmer them for about thirty minutes, or until the desired color change has taken place.

Some of the substances used as mordants are listed below together with their characteristics, and directions for their use on animal, and vegetable, fiber yarns.

ALUM: There are different kinds of alum. Aluminium potassium sulfate is the kind most commonly used in vegetable dyeing, but other kinds can be used with fairly satisfactory results. Either the granular or powdered form may be used, and it can be purchased from chemical companies, from some vegetable dye companies and in, or by special order from, drug stores. This type of alum is fairly inexpensive and a pound of it will mordant four to five pounds of yarns. It should be stored in a dry place. If too much alum is used it will make yarns sticky and gummy, so watch the amounts. Alum gives best results when used as a mordant before the yarns are dyed; however, it gives fair to good results when mixed with the dye bath. It is good for all fibers.

To mordant animal fibers with alum: For one pound of dry fibers, put three gallons of warm water in a four to five gallon size enamel container, add three ounces of alum and stir until completely dissolved. (One and a half tablespoons alum equals approximately one ounce of alum.) Add the wet, scoured fibers and simmer them for one hour. After they are cool, and the fibers have been rinsed, they are ready for dyeing. Wool yarns can be rolled in towels and kept damp for a few days, or refrigerated and kept damp for several days before dyeing; silk should be dried or dyed immediately. It must be understood that alum does not change the color of the fibers; the yarns turn the dye bath the color the bath would be without the use of any mordant. For example, alum mordanted yarns will dye yellow from goldenrod blossom, brass or gold from chrome mordant, and dark green from copperas mordant.

To mordant vegetable fibers with alum: For one pound of dry vegetable fibers, put three gallons of warm water in a four or five gallon enamel container, add four ounces of alum and one fourth of a cup of sal soda and stir this mixture until it is completely dissolved. The wet, scoured fibers can then be added and should be boiled for one to two hours, depending on whether the fibers are coarse or fine, large or small. Cool the fibers; rinse them; dry or dye.

BLUE VITRIOL: Blue vitriol, commonly known as bluestone, is copper sulfate. It can be purchased in lump and crystal form from drug and farm supply stores in packages; the amount can be as small as four ounces. If this mordant is needed in large amounts, it can be purchased from chemical companies and from some vegetable dye supply companies. It is fairly inexpensive and four ounces will mordant one to three pounds of fibers, depending on the desired depth of the dyed color. Blue vitriol colors fibers green, and this is a good mordant if one wants to add greenish tones to the colors. It works best for wool fibers, fair to good for silk and some vegetable fibers. Good results can be obtained from any of the mordanting methods.

To mordant animal fibers with blue vitriol: For one pound of animal fibers, put three gallons of warm water in an enamel container, then add two ounces of blue vitriol and dissolve it completely. The wet, scoured yarns can then be added and these should simmer for about one hour in order to produce a dark green, a little less for lighter shades. Cool the yarns, rinse them and they may be dyed or dried.

To mordant vegetable fibers with blue vitriol: For one pound of vegetable fibers, put three gallons of warm water in an enamel container, add three to four ounces of blue vitriol, depending on the coarseness of the fibers. Now add the wet, scoured yarns and boil them for one to two hours; again, this varies with the coarseness of the fibers. The yarns may now be cooled, rinsed, and dried or dyed.

CHROME: There is more than one kind of chrome, but potassium dichromate, in granular form, is the one commonly used in vegetable dyeing. It is called bichromate of potash—dichromate and bichromate are the same. Chrome colors yarns in a range from tan to orange and will make gold, brass, and rust colors.

Potassium dichromate is expensive but as little as half a pound goes a long way in mordanting. It can be purchased from chemical companies and from some vegetable dye companies, or by special order through some drug stores.

Since chrome is very sensitive to light, the container should be kept covered during the mordanting process. If light gets to the mordanting fibers, they will turn green, and green tones will appear, instead of yellow ones, in the dyed yarns. The granular chrome should be stored in a dry container from which all light is sealed off. Most important, chrome is poison; do please avoid inhaling the fumes.

Chrome gives best results when used as a mordant before the yarns are dyed, and is good with all fibers, excellent for wool.

To mordant animal fibers with chrome: For one pound of animal fiber yarns, put three gallons of warm water in an enamel container, add one tablespoon of chrome and dissolve completely. Now add the wet, scoured yarns, cover the container immediately, and simmer for one hour. The yarns should be cooled in the covered container and then rinsed. It is preferable to dye the yarns immediately. It's not absolutely essential to cover the dye bath container, but it is a good precaution. If the yarns must be dried, dry away from strong light, store in a dark place.

To mordant vegetable fibers with chrome: For one pound of vegetable fiber yarns, put three gallons of warm water in an enamel container, add one tablespoon of chrome for light color, two tablespoons for dark color, and dissolve completely. Wet, scoured yarns, can now be added. Cover the container; boil for one to two hours, depending on the coarseness of the fibers; cool the yarns in the covered container; rinse. It is preferable to dye the yarns immediately. Again, it is not essential to cover the dye bath container. If the yarns must be dried, dry them away from strong light and store them out of light.

COPPERAS: Copperas is iron or ferrous sulfate. It is inexpensive and can be purchased in drug and farm supply stores in packaged amounts as small as four ounces. It can be purchased in larger quantities from chemical companies and from some vegetable dye companies. Four ounces will mordant two to four pounds of yarns. Copperas darkens the fibers and produces greens, purples, and blacks from certain dyestuffs. However, too much copperas streaks and injures fibers. As a mordant for wool and some vegetable fibers it works very well, although it often works poorly for silk. It will give shades that are darker when used in the dye bath while the yarns are dyeing. Lighter shades can usually be obtained when the mordanting is done before the yarns are dyed. Note that too much copperas will produce a bronzed effect in black.

To mordant animal fibers with copperas: To prepare the dye bath use two and a half to three gallons of dye bath liquid for one pound of animal fiber yarns. Three ounces of copperas should be added to the dye bath (two tablespoons equals approximately one ounce) and it should be stirred until completely dissolved. Then add the wet, scoured yarns and simmer for thirty minutes. When this is completed dissolve four tablespoons of tartaric acid, and half a cup of Glauber's salts, in one pint of hot water, and add this mixture to the dye bath. Simmer another thirty minutes. The yarns should be cooled in the dye and mordant bath and then rinsed in warm water until the rinse is clear. Shake water from the yarns and hang in the shade to dry.

To mordant vegetable fibers with copperas: To prepare the bath use three gallons of dye bath liquid for one pound of vegetable fibers. Add four ounces of copperas to this and stir until completely dissolved. The wet, scoured yarns should be added and boiled for about one hour. Then dissolve four tablespoons tartaric acid and half a cup of Glauber's salts in one pint of hot water and add it to the mordant-dye bath. Boil for another thirty minutes. The yarns should be cooled in the dye bath, rinsed until the rinse is clear, and all water should then be removed from the yarns. Hang the yarns in the shade to dry. It's difficult to mordant and dye coarse, large hard twist linen yarns.

TANNIC ACID: Tannic acid is also referred to as tannin and it turns fibers tan to brown. This should be taken into consideration when selecting the colors to be dyed over tannic acid mordanted fibers. It works especially well with tans and brown dyes on vegetable fibers.

The colors dyed from tannic acid mordanted yarns have a tendency to become darker with age. Also, some barks, galls, leaves, and twigs have a natural supply of tannic acid in them; sumac, in particular, is a good natural source of tannic acid. Yarns can be mordanted by using parts of the sumac tree, but only the red berry variety should be used as the white berry variety is deadly poison. The red berry sumac also makes dyes, and other mordants can be used with this dye.

The fluffy, powdered tannic acid can be purchased from chemical companies and by special order through drug stores. It is fairly expensive but a little goes a long way. One fourth of a pound will more than fill a pint size fruit jar and will mordant several pounds of yarns. Tannic acid should be stored in a dry place, in a light tight container. Oxgalls and nutgalls are sold by vegetable dye suppliers for the same use as tannic acid; they both contain tannic acid and can be used instead of the powder.

To mordant animal fibers with tannic acid: For one pound of dry animal fiber yarns, put three gallons of warm water in an enamel container, add four tablespoons tannic acid and dissolve. Now immerse the wet, scoured yarns in this mixture and simmer for one hour. Cool yarns in the mordant, then rinse them, dye or dry.

When tannic acid is used with the dye bath, add the same amount to the dye bath before the yarns are put in, then follow the standard dyeing recipe.

To mordant vegetable fibers with tannic acid: For one pound of dry vegetable fiber yarns, put three gallons of warm water in an enamel container, add eight tablespoons of tannic acid and dissolve. The wet scoured yarns should then be added and boiled gently. If the fibers are small and fine, boil them for one hour and allow two hours for large coarse fibers. Cool the yarns in the mordant. The vegetable fibers can be left in this mordant overnight. Finally, rinse; dye or dry.

When tannic acid is used with the dye bath, add the same amount to the dye bath before the yarns are put in, then follow the standard dyeing recipe.

TIN: Tin is stannous chloride, and the crystal or powder form can be used. Again, it is expensive but a little goes a long way—one fourth of a pound of tin will mordant several pounds of yarns. It can be purchased from chemical companies and from some vegetable dye supply companies or by special order through some drug stores.

Tin is a good mordant for animal fibers, fair to good for some of the soft twist vegetable fibers, but is often poor for linen. It makes bright colors, and is especially good for reds and yellows. It is best to use tin in mordanting before the yarns are dyed. However, it can be used to brighten colors after they have been mordanted with another mordant and dyed—the first mordant color will not be changed, only brightened.

To mordant animal fibers and soft vegetable fibers with tin: For one pound of dry fibers, put three gallons of warm water in an enamel container, add two teaspoons of tin and dissolve thoroughly. The wet, scoured fibers should now be added and allowed to simmer for one hour. If a cover is placed over the container, it will reduce fumes in the working area. Let the yarns cool in the mordant, then rinse, dry or dye.

To brighten colors after they have been dyed: Yarns that have been dyed with any of the other mordants may be brightened with tin. To do this, put three gallons of warm water in an enamel container for one pound of dry dyed yarns, add one teaspoon of tin and dissolve thoroughly. Simmer the wet, dyed yarn in this mixture for fifteen to thirty minutes. The simmering time will depend on the coarseness and the size of the fibers. The mixture can now be cooled, but do not allow fibers to remain in it until it becomes cold. Rinse the fibers once in mild soap.

DYEING FIBERS

The dye bath: The dye bath is the liquid in which the dyestuffs are boiled. It should be lukewarm when the yarns are put into it and of a sufficient amount to completely·cover the yarns. If additional water is added to the dye bath, it will make the colors dye lighter shades. Two and a half to three gallons of dye bath is usually enough liquid to dye a pound of yarn. Tartaric acid and Glauber's salts must be added to the dye bath at the mid-point of the dyeing process.

For the recipes in this book the dye baths are made by extracting the color from the dyestuffs with boiling water but the process varies slightly. In some, the dyestuffs are covered with water, and boiled until the color is transferred from the dyestuffs to the water. In others, the dyestuffs are soaked, and then boiled in the soaking water. When powders are used, they can be made into water based pastes and allowed to set for different lengths of time, before mixing with water and boiling. Or, other powders can be put into cloth bags, covered with about three gallons of water, soaked, and then boiled in the soaking water.

The length of time it takes for soaking and removing the color depends on the type and condition of the dyestuffs.

Dyeing yarns: The yarns should be thoroughly wet when they are put into the lukewarm dye bath. Raise the temperature of the dye bath to a simmer temperature, which is 180° to 210° F. and begin to time the bath. This temperature should be maintained about twenty minutes for light shades of color, and thirty minutes for dark shades of color. The recipes that follow are for the medium dark shades.

Dissolve four tablespoons of tartaric acid and half a cup of Glauber's salts in one pint of hot water, lift the yarns out of the dye bath and pour in the dissolved tartaric acid and Glauber's salts. Mix this well into the bath and then return the yarns to the mixture and simmer or boil them another twenty to thirty minutes. The time will depend on the kind of fibers of the yarns, and the desired shade of color. If the yarns are cooled in the dye bath it will darken the colors; this is especially true for cotton.

Tartaric acid and Glauber's salts are part of the standard recipes for dyeing yarns. Tartaric acid and the commercial cream of tartar give the same results, and it is used to make bright clear colors. If the yarns are dyed without it, and they can be, they will lack luster. Cream of tartar can be purchased in grocery stores and drug stores, and tartaric acid may be purchased from chemical companies and from some vegetable dye supply companies—either one is fairly inexpensive.

The Glauber's salts are used as a leveling agent; it exhausts the color from the dye bath and makes for uniform dyeing. If Glauber's salts are used it's unnecessary to constantly stir the bath while the yarns are dyeing, and this whole process is eliminated. Although yarns can be dyed without Glauber's salts, it's not to be recommended. Also, the salts are inexpensive when purchased from chemical companies in one and two hundred pound quantities. It is expensive to purchase the salts by the pound from drug stores.

The first rinse after the yarns have been dyed should be almost the same temperature as the dye bath the yarns were taken from. Three rinses are usually enough, ending with a rinse of lukewarm temperature.

All yarns should be dried out of direct heat and light—they can be dried outside in the shade or inside at room temperature. Don't use a clothes dryer. However, the yarns will dry faster if their drip direction is rearranged.

If the dye doesn't turn out well, it can sometimes be corrected by putting the yarns back in the same dye bath and simmering them for another fifteen minutes to one hour. The faulty dye can also be top dyed with another color and this will often turn out well.

A few other tips—one fourth of a cup of white vinegar per gallon of water or half a teaspoon acetic acid in the last rinse will soften wool. A mild soap rinse can sometimes brighten colors that have been dyed yellow and red with a tin mordant. As far as cleaning up is concerned, any commercial household powdered cleanser will remove dye and mordant stains from pots and pans.

LEVELING DYE LOTS

Glauber's salts will level dye lots. When yarns are dyed from the same dyestuff, at different times, they can be made the same shade by simmering them in a Glauber's salts bath. However, the colors may be slightly dulled.

To level dye lots with Glauber's salts: Dissolve one cup of Glauber's salts in one quart of hot water for each pound of the dry yarns that have to be leveled. Add the dissolved Glauber's salts to enough warm water to comfortably cover the batch of yarn; add the wet yarns; simmer for thirty minutes to one hour, depending on the amount of difference between the shades of color. Rinse the yarns and hang them out of direct light to dry.

COLOR FASTNESS

There are tests for color fastness, and these may be made in a number of ways. These tests are made for light or sun fastness, and for water fastness. The need for a test for bleeding and crocking is eliminated by using Glauber's salts in the dye baths.

To test vegetable dyed yarns for sun and light fastness, just expose a piece of the yarns to direct sunlight, or artificial light, for certain periods of time, and then compare it with another piece of the same yarn which has received no light. For example, part of a skein can be hung outside in the sun, while another part of the skein is kept in a paper bag for the same length of time. The results should be compared and recorded by weeks or months.

To test for water fastness, a piece of the dyed yarn can be washed under ordinary washing conditions and then compared with an unwashed piece of the same yarn. However, it is much better to dry clean vegetable dyed fabrics than to wash them.

II. Vegetable Dye Recipes

These dye recipes are listed by color range instead of by color because the hues produced by vegetable dyes do not match the hues produced by aniline dyes. Nor do shades of vegetable dyes fall into specific categories in color charts. If vegetable dyes were the same as aniline dyes, it would be pointless to make them.

Each person who follows any recipe in this book will more than likely create a shade of color that's a little different from anyone else's because of conditions he cannot control. The time of year when the dyestuff is collected perhaps most influences the final color. The amount of moisture during a season, the number of daylight hours, and the type of soil where the plant grows are also factors that will affect its dye properties. Generally, parts of the plant above ground need a lot of sunshine to produce strong dyes. Barks may be an exception. And each dyer's individual difference in measurements, in the composition of the water, in timing, and in temperature contribute to preventing uniformity of color.

It follows that the color of each vegetable dye is unique.

III. Reds and Pinks

Some of the dye materials for colors ranging from reds to pinks can be found growing in your own geographical area; others must be purchased from commercial sources. Pokeweed berries, bloodroot, and other red dye materials grow wild. Cochineal, madder, alkanet and cudbear can be purchased commercially.

The fiber being dyed influences the final shade of red: vegetable fibers normally dye lighter shades than animal fibers. Pinks for animal fibers can often be obtained by diluting a red dye.

The permanence of a color is determined by the dye substance.

1. BLOODROOT WITH TIN MORDANT

The bloodroot plant can be found growing wild in many sections of the country. The dried roots can be purchased from commercial suppliers, but fresh roots make brighter dyes.

Ingredients:

1 pound wool yarn, previously mordanted with tin
1 pound fresh bloodroots
4 tablespoons tartaric acid
½ cup Glauber's salts

To make dye bath: Cut the roots into 1" to 3" lengths, place in an enamel container, cover with two and a half gallons of warm water and soak for twelve hours. After soaking, simmer the roots in the same water in which the roots have been soaked for about two hours. Cool. Remove the refuse, and the liquid becomes the dye bath.

To dye wool yarn: Add the wet, tin mordanted, wool yarn to the dye bath and simmer for thirty minutes. Dissolve four tablespoons of tartaric acid and half a cup of Glauber's salts in one pint of hot water and add this mixture to the dye bath. Simmer another thirty minutes. Cool. Rinse the wool yarn in warm water until the rinse is clear. Finally, squeeze all the water out of the yarn and hang it in the shade to dry.

Color: This recipe makes a color range of reds and pinks. The lighter shades may be obtained by using the dye bath a second and third time. The colors are fast.

Alternate fibers: Although wool dyes best, other natural fibers can be dyed fairly well.

29

2. COCHINEAL WITH ALUM MORDANT

In this cochineal recipe for red, the mordant is alum.

Ingredients:

1 pound wool yarn, previously mordanted with alum
½ pound powdered cochineal
4 tablespoons tartaric acid
½ cup Glauber's salts

To make dye bath: Mix the cochineal powder with enough warm water to make a thin paste. Make certain to use an enamel or glass container that is larger than you appear to need because the mixture will thicken and expand. Let the mixture set for about twelve hours and stir three or four times. After the twelve hours, transfer the mixture to a five gallon enamel container. Slowly add three gallons of warm water, stirring to dissolve lumps and thick masses of powder in the mixture. Heat, then simmer for about ten minutes. This is the dye bath.

To dye wool yarn: Add the wet, alum mordanted wool yarn to the dye bath and simmer for about thirty minutes. Dissolve four tablespoons of tartaric acid and half a cup of Glauber's salts in one pint of hot water and add this to the dye bath. Simmer for another thirty minutes. Cool. Rinse in warm water until the rinse is clear. Shake out the water and hang in the shade to dry.

Color: This recipe makes a purple-red and the color is fast. The dye bath may be used again and until the color is gone. Each successive dyeing will give a lighter shade than the one before it.

Alternate fibers: Silk fibers dye well. Linen and cotton dye lighter shades than wool and silk. Mohair dyes well.

3. COCHINEAL WITH TIN MORDANT

The insect from which cochineal is made is not native to the United States; therefore the dye substance has to be purchased from natural dye supply companies. It is available in powder form, ready for use. Some suppliers stock two colors of cochineal—ruby and carmine red. It is one of the most dependable red dye substances.

Ingredients:

1 pound wool yarn, previously mordanted with tin
1 pound powdered cochineal
4 tablespoons tartaric acid
½ cup Glauber's salts

To make dye bath: Mix the cochineal powder with enough warm water to make a thin paste.
Make certain to use an enamel or glass container that is larger than you appear to need because the mixture will thicken and expand. Let the mixture set for about twelve hours, stirring it occasionally. Transfer the mixture to a five gallon enamel

container. Slowly add three gallons of warm water, stirring to dissolve all lumps and thick masses in the mixture. Heat and then simmer for about ten minutes. This is the dye bath.

To dye wool yarn: Add the wet, tin mordanted wool yarn to the dye bath and simmer for about thirty minutes. Dissolve four tablespoons of tartaric acid and half a cup of Glauber's salts in one pint of hot water and add to the dye bath. Simmer for another thirty minutes. Cool. Rinse in warm water until the rinse is clear. Shake out the water and hang in the shade to dry.

Color: This recipe makes a bright red and the color is fast. The dye bath may be used again and until the color is gone. Each time the dye bath is used the color will be lighter.

Alternate fibers: Silk fibers dye very well. Linen and cotton dye lighter shades than wool and silk.

4. CRAB APPLES WITH ALUM MORDANT

Pick the crab apples when they are red in color and ripe.

Ingredients:

1 pound wool yarn, previously mordanted with alum
4 gallons red, ripe, ornamental crab apples
4 tablespoons tartaric acid
½ cup Glauber's salts

To make dye bath: Place the crab apples in a five gallon enamel container, cover them with water and boil until the apples are soft. Cool. Strain. The liquid has now become the dye bath.

To dye wool yarn: Add the wet, alum mordanted wool yarn to the dye bath and simmer for thirty minutes. Dissolve four tablespoons of tartaric acid and half a cup of Glauber's salts in one pint of hot water and add this mixture to the dye bath. Simmer another thirty minutes. Cool the wool yarn in the dye bath. Rinse in warm water until the rinse is clear. The last rinse should be in warm water which has had about one fourth cup of vinegar per gallon added to it, as this will help to remove sugar or any sticky feeling from the yarn. Finally, shake all water from the yarn and hang it in the shade to dry.

Color: This recipe makes shades of pink, and it is fairly fast.

Alternate fibers: Silk fibers will respond to this dye process in about the same way as wool. However, the color is too light for vegetable fibers.

5. CUDBEAR WITH ALUM MORDANT

Cudbear powder can be purchased from commercial sources. This dyestuff is made from lichens. However, making dyes from lichens can be a separate area of vegetable dyeing, and dyes made from other types of lichens are not included in this book. This one is included because of its beauty and commercial availability.

Ingredients:

1 pound of wool yarn, previously mordanted with alum
4 ounces powdered cudbear
4 tablespoons tartaric acid
½ cup Glauber's salts

To make dye bath: Mix four ounces of cudbear with one quart of warm water in a glass or an enamel container. Stir and mix until the powder has completely dissolved into a thin paste. Put three gallons warm water in another enamel container and add the mixture a little at a time. Stir with the hand and rub any remaining lumps of powder between the fingers to dissolve them. Heat to simmer and keep the mixture simmering at the same heat for fifteen minutes. After this, again stir the mixture well. This is the dye bath.

To dye wool yarn: Add the wet, alum mordanted wool yarn to the dye bath and simmer for twenty minutes. Dissolve four tablespoons of tartaric acid and half a cup of Glauber's salts in one pint of hot water and add this mixture to the dye bath. Simmer another twenty minutes. Cool. Rinse in warm water until the rinse is clear. Shake water from the yarn and hang it in the shade to dry.

Color: This recipe makes shades of wine red and the colors are fast. The dye bath can be used three or four times for lighter shades of red.

Alternate fibers: This dyestuff is excellent for all natural fibers—linen, cotton, and some silk may, however, dye lighter shades than wool and jute.

6. LAVENDER AND ROSEMARY EXTRACT WITH ALUM MORDANT

Pharmaceutical extracts of plants often make rare shades of color, and old stocks of drugs are good sources of supply. This particular extract not only yields an exotic color, but also gives a permanent perfume to the fibers. The recipe may be divided into smaller amounts if desired; one fourth of this recipe will dye four ounces of yarn.

Ingredients:

1 pound wool yarn, previously mordanted with alum
8 ounces fluid extract of lavender and rosemary
4 tablespoons tartaric acid
½ cup Glauber's salts

To make dye bath: Pour eight ounces of extract of lavender and rosemary in a five gallon enamel container. Stir in about three gallons of warm water and heat to simmer temperature. This is the dye bath.

To dye wool yarn: Add the wet, alum mordanted wool yarn to the dye bath and simmer for thirty minutes. Dissolve four tablespoons of tartaric acid and half a cup of Glauber's salts in one pint of hot water and add to the dye bath. Simmer another thirty minutes. Cool yarn in the dye bath. Rinse in warm water until the rinse is clear, then shake the water from the yarn and hang it in the shade to dry.

Color: This recipe makes a dark dusty rose color that is fast. The color from the dye bath was exhausted with one dyeing.

Alternate fibers: No other fibers were tested.

7. MADDER (POWDER FORM NO. 1) WITH ALUM MORDANT

Madder is not grown in quantity in this country but can be purchased from commercial natural dye companies. This variation of the previous recipe calls for alum as a mordant.

Ingredients:

1 pound wool yarn, previously mordanted with alum
½ pound madder in powder form
4 tablespoons tartaric acid
½ cup Glauber's salts

To make dye bath: Place half a pound of powdered madder in a one gallon enamel or glass container and add enough water to make a thin paste. Let the mixture soak for about twelve hours. It will thicken and expand during this time. After soaking, transfer the mixture to a five gallon enamel container and add three and a half gallons of water. Stir until all thick masses of powder are dissolved. Heat the liquid to a simmer temperature (180° to 200°F.) and hold there for ten to fifteen minutes. Do not boil the liquid; boiling will bring out the yellow dye substance in the madder. Cool. This is the dye bath.

To dye wool yarn: Add the wet, alum mordanted wool yarn to the dye bath and hold at about 180°F. for twenty minutes or until the desired shade of red is obtained. Dissolve four tablespoons of tartaric acid and half a cup Glauber's salts in one pint of hot water and add to the dye bath. Hold at 180°F. for another twenty minutes. Cool. Rinse the yarn in warm water until the rinse is clear, then shake the water from the yarn and hang it in the shade to dry.

Color: This recipe makes a red that is color fast. The dye bath may be used again for lighter shades.

Alternate fibers: Silk fibers dye well. Linen and cotton fibers dye lighter shades than do wool and silk. Mohair dyes very well.

8. MADDER (POWDER FORM NO. 2) WITH TIN MORDANT

Madder in powder form is sold by suppliers of natural dyestuffs.

Ingredients:

1 pound wool yarn, previously mordanted with tin
½ pound madder in powder form
4 tablespoons tartaric acid
½ cup Glauber's salts

To make dye bath: Place half a pound of powdered madder in a one gallon enamel or glass container and add enough water to make a thin paste. Let the mixture soak for about twelve hours. It will expand and thicken during this time. After soaking, transfer the mixture to a five gallon enamel container and stir in three and a half gallons of water. Mix until all thick masses of powder are dissolved. Heat the liquid to a simmer (180° to 200°F.) and hold there for about ten minutes. Do not boil the liquid; boiling will bring out the yellow dye substance in the madder. Cool. This is the dye bath.

To dye wool yarn: Add the wet, tin mordanted wool yarn to the dye bath and hold the temperature just under the simmering point for about twenty minutes. Dissolve four tablespoons of tartaric acid and half a cup of Glauber's salts in one pint of hot water and add to the dye bath. Hold just under simmer for another twenty minutes. Cool. Rinse in warm water until the rinse is clear. Shake the water from the yarn and hang it in the shade to dry.

Color: This tin mordant recipe makes a red that is much brighter than the red that results when alum mordant is used. The dye bath can be used again for lighter shades. The color is fast.

Alternate fibers: Silk fibers dye well. Vegetable fibers dye well but in lighter shades than the colors that are produced on wool and silk.

9. MADDER (ROOTS) WITH ALUM MORDANT

Madder roots are sold commercially. The preparation and use of a madder dye bath is a very sensitive procedure, whether you use madder in root or powder form. The roots contain red and yellow dye substances. When boiled, the red is lost. Long and hard boiling turns madder roots (and the dye bath) black and makes an unsatisfactory dye.

Ingredients:

1 pound wool yarn, previously mordanted with alum
1 pound madder roots
4 tablespoons tartaric acid
½ cup Glauber's salts

To make dye bath: Cut the madder roots into ¼" to ½" lengths and place in a five gallon enamel container. Cover with three and a half gallons of water and soak for twelve hours. The roots will expand and absorb some of the water. At the end of twelve hours, add one gallon of water to the soaking mixture and simmer for about forty-five minutes. Cool. Remove the roots. The liquid becomes the dye bath.

To dye wool yarn: Add the wet, alum mordanted wool yarn to the dye bath and simmer fifteen to twenty minutes, depending on the shade desired. Dissolve four tablespoons of tartaric acid and half a cup of Glauber's salts in one pint of hot water and add to the dye bath. Simmer another fifteen to twenty minutes. Cool. Rinse in warm water until the rinse is clear. Shake the water from the yarn and hang in the shade to dry.

Color: This recipe makes red and the color is fast. The dye bath may be used again and again as long as it contains color. Each dyeing will give a lighter shade than the previous one.

Alternate fibers: Silk fibers dye well. Linen and cotton dye lighter shades than wool and silk.

10. POKEWEED BERRIES WITH ALUM MORDANT

Pokeweek berries should be picked late in the summer after they have turned dark purple. They can be used fresh or stored frozen.

Ingredients:

1 pound wool yarn, previously mordanted with alum
4 gallons pokeweed berries on stems
4 tablespoons tartaric acid
½ cup Glauber's salts

To make dye bath: Cut the pokeweed berries and stems into 1" to 3" lengths. Place in a five gallon enamel container, cover with water, and boil for about forty-five minutes. Crushing the berries while they boil will release more dye. Cool. Remove all solid matter, and the liquid becomes the dye bath.

To dye wool yarn: Add the wet, alum mordanted wool yarn to the dye bath; simmer for thirty minutes. Dissolve four tablespoons of tartaric acid and half a cup of Glauber's salts in one pint of hot water and add to the dye bath. Simmer thirty minutes longer. Cool. Rinse the yarn in warm water until the rinse is clear, then shake the water from the yarn and hang it in the shade to dry.

Color: This recipe makes shades of red and fades from sunlight, but the color does not disappear entirely. The dye bath may be used more than one time.

Alternate fibers: Silk dyes red, cotton and linen dye pink.

11. POKEWEED BERRIES WITH TIN MORDANT

Pokeweed berries should be picked late in the summer after they have turned to a dark purple color. They can be used fresh, or frozen for later use. The dried pokeweed berries make shades of brown.

Ingredients:

1 pound wool yarn, previously mordanted with tin
4 gallons fresh pokeweed berries on stems
4 tablespoons tartaric acid
½ cup Glauber's salts

To make dye bath: Cut the pokeweed berries and stems into 1" to 3" lengths, place in a five gallon enamel container, cover with water, and boil for about forty-five minutes. Crush berries while cooking to obtain all the color substance. Cool. Strain. The liquid is the dye bath.

To dye wool yarn: Add the wet, tin mordanted, wool yarn to the dye bath; simmer for thirty minutes. Dissolve four tablespoons of tartaric acid and half a cup of Glauber's salts in one pint of hot water and add this mixture to the dye bath. Simmer another thirty minutes. Cool. Rinse the yarn in warm water until the rinse is clear. Shake all the water from the yarn and hang it in the shade to dry.

Color: This recipe makes a red that has a yellow tone and the color will fade to some extent. However, yarn dyed with pokeweed berries will not lose its color completely and it is a good base for top dyeing. The dye bath may be used more than one time.

Alternate fibers: Silk fibers will dye to about the same shades as wool. Linen and cotton will dye to shades of pink.

12. SCARLET SAGE BLOSSOMS WITH ALUM MORDANT

The scarlet sage plant is also called salvia. The growing season will affect the amount of pigment in scarlet sage blossoms; extended hot weather is best for blossoms to be used for making the dye and they should be used only after the blossoms have reached maturity. The blossoms may be used fresh or dried and stored for later use.

Ingredients:

1 pound of wool yarn, previously mordanted with alum
4 gallons scarlet sage blossoms
4 tablespoons tartaric acid
½ cup Glauber's salts

To make dye bath: Pick the blossoms from their stems, place them in a five gallon enamel container, and cover them with water. Boil for about thirty minutes. Cool. Remove the blossoms and the liquid becomes the dye bath.

To dye wool yarn: Add the wet, alum mordanted, wool yarn to the dye bath and simmer for thirty minutes. Dissolve four tablespoons of tartaric acid and half a cup of Glauber's salts in one pint of hot water and add this mixture to the dye bath. Simmer another thirty minutes. Cool. Rinse the yarn in warm water until the rinse is clear. Squeeze all the water out of the yarn and hang it in the shade to dry.

Color: This recipe makes various shades of dusty rose; the colors will fade to some extent.

Alternate fibers: Silk fibers dye very well, sometimes better than wool. Linen and cotton fibers do not dye satisfactorily.

IV. Yellows, Golds, and Brasses

Dye substances for making yellows, golds, and brasses abound in most geographical locations and they may also be obtained from commercial suppliers.

The shades of color that can be achieved from growing substances will be largely determined by the season in which the materials are cut. For instance, spring and early summer cuttings often give shades of yellow, but late summer and fall cuttings from the same plant will give golds and brasses.

Mordants, of course, affect the color and frequently change it.

13. ANNATTO AND RED ONION SKINS WITH TIN MORDANT

Annatto is a dye substance and it can be purchased from vegetable dye supply companies. It is sometimes used for coloring cheese, butter, and varnishes.

To make this dye, equal parts of dyes of approximately the same strength, made separately from annatto and red onion skins, have to be combined.

Ingredients:

1 pound wool yarn, previously mordanted with tin
2 gallons of red onion skins
½ pound powdered annatto
4 tablespoons tartaric acid
½ cup Glauber's salts.

To make the first half of dye bath: Tie the annatto in a cheesecloth bag, place it in a three to four gallon enamel container, cover it with about two gallons of warm water and let it soak for about twelve hours. The bag should be large enough to leave space for the powdered annatto to expand when it becomes wet, and it should be boiled in the same water in which it has been soaked for about two hours. Cool. Remove the bag. The liquid is now half of the dye bath.

To make the second half of dye bath: Place two gallons of red onion skins in an enamel container, cover them with about two gallons of water and boil until the skins are clear. Cool. Remove the skins. The liquid is now the second half of the dye bath. The final step is to combine the two dyes in a five gallon enamel container.

To dye wool yarn: Add the wet, tin mordanted, wool yarn to the dye bath and simmer for thirty minutes. Dissolve four tablespoons of tartaric acid and half a cup of Glauber's salts in one pint of hot water and add this mixture to the dye bath. Simmer the dye bath and the mixture for another thirty minutes, or until the color is as dark as desired. Cool. Rinse the wool yarn in warm water until the rinse is clear. Squeeze all the water from the yarn and hang it in the shade to dry.

Color: This recipe makes a bright dark yellow color which has good fastness. The dye bath may be used more than one time to produce lighter shades.

Alternate fibers: Silk yarns will dye well in this bath. Linen and cotton yarns also respond to the dye but the color it produces will be much lighter than that of silk and wool.

14. BUTTERFLY WEED BLOSSOMS WITH ALUM MORDANT

Gather the butterfly weed blossoms when they are in full bloom and use fresh blossoms to make the dye bath.

Ingredients:

1 pound silk yarn, previously mordanted with alum
4 gallons butterfly weed blossoms
4 tablespoons tartaric acid
½ cup Glauber's salts

To make dye bath: Place the butterfly weed blossoms in a five gallon enamel container, cover it with water and boil for about forty-five minutes. Cool. Remove the cooked blossoms. The liquid has now become the dye bath.

To dye silk yarn: Add the wet, alum mordanted, silk yarn to the dye bath and simmer it for thirty minutes. Dissolve four tablespoons of tartaric acid and half a cup of Glauber's salts in one pint of hot water and add to the dye bath. Simmer the mixture in the dye bath for another thirty minutes. Allow the yarn to cool in the dye bath. Rinse in warm water until rinse is clear. Shake all the water from the yarn and hang in the shade to dry.

Color: This recipe makes shades of yellow and the color is reasonably fast.

Alternate fibers: The recipe is suitable for all natural fibers. However, vegetable fibers will dye lighter shades of color than animal fibers.

15. CHRYSANTHEMUM BLOSSOMS WITH ALUM MORDANT

The red, yellow, and bronze chrysanthemum blossoms will produce shades of yellow, and they may be combined to make one dye. The blossoms can be used fresh or dried in the sun or a slow oven for later use. The blossoms should be picked when they are in full bloom.

Ingredients:

1 pound wool yarn, previously mordanted with alum
4 gallons chrysanthemum blossoms
4 tablespoons tartaric acid
½ cup Glauber's salts

To make dye bath: Place four gallons of chrysanthemum blossoms in a five gallon enamel container, cover with water and boil for about forty-five minutes. Cool. Remove the refuse, and the liquid becomes the dye bath.

To dye wool yarn: Add the wet, alum mordanted, wool yarn to the dye bath and simmer for thirty minutes. Dissolve four tablespoons of tartaric acid and half a cup of Glauber's salts in one pint of hot water, add this mixture to the dye bath and simmer another thirty minutes. Cool. Rinse the yarn in warm water until the rinse is clear. Shake the water from the yarn and hang it in the shade to dry.

Color: This recipe makes various shades of yellow and the color is fast. The dye bath may be used again to make lighter shades.

Alternate fibers: Silk fibers dye well. It is difficult to obtain good shades of yellow with linen and cotton fibers from the recipe.

16. CHRYSANTHEMUM BLOSSOMS AND MARIGOLD BLOSSOMS WITH ALUM MORDANT

When there are not enough blossoms of one kind available, these two types of blossoms can be mixed. For this recipe, any variety of either plant is satisfactory.

Ingredients:

1 pound wool yarn, previously mordanted with alum
2 gallons chrysanthemum blossoms
2 gallons marigold blossoms
4 tablespoons tartaric acid
½ cup Glauber's salts

To make dye bath: Place the combined blossoms in a five gallon enamel container, cover with water and boil for about forty-five minutes. Cool. Remove the refuse. The liquid is now the dye bath.

To dye wool yarn: Add the wet, alum mordanted, wool yarn to the dye bath and simmer for thirty minutes. Dissolve four tablespoons of tartaric acid and half a cup of Glauber's salts in one pint of hot water and add to the dye bath. Simmer another thirty minutes. Cool. Rinse in warm water until the rinse is clear. Shake water from the yarn and hang in the shade to dry.

Color: This recipe will produce various shades of brass. These may vary according to different combinations of the two varieties of blossoms. The color is fast.

Alternate fibers: Silk fibers will dye very well. Linen and cotton dye to a very light yellow.

17. COCKLEBUR WITH ALUM MORDANT

Cockleburs should be picked in late summer and can be used fresh or dried for later use.

Ingredients:

1 pound wool yarn, previously mordanted with alum
4 gallons cockleburs
4 tablespoons tartaric acid
½ cup Glauber's salts

To make dye bath: Cut the cockleburs from their stalks, place them in a five gallon enamel container, cover with water and allow to soak for twelve hours. After twelve hours boil the cockleburs in the water in which they have been soaked for about two hours. Add extra water as it boils away. Cool. Remove the cooked cockleburs. The liquid is now the dye bath.

To dye wool yarn: Add the wet, alum mordanted, wool yarn to the dye bath and simmer it for thirty minutes. Dissolve four tablespoons of tartaric acid and half a cup of Glauber's salts in one pint of hot water and add this mixture to the dye bath. Simmer the dye bath and the mixture for another thirty minutes. Cool. Rinse the wool yarn in warm water until the rinse is clear. Shake the water from the yarn and hang it in the shade to dry.

Color: This recipe makes a brass color and the color is fast. The dye bath may be used again for lighter shades.

Alternate fibers: Silk fibers and soft spun cotton fibers dye well. Linen fibers do not dye.

18. DAHLIA BLOSSOMS WITH ALUM MORDANT

The red, pink, and yellow dahlia blossoms will produce a dye of various shades of yellow. Seasonal conditions and soil may also have an effect on the color. The blossoms should be cut when they are in full bloom. They may be used fresh, or dried in a slow oven or in the sun and kept for later use. Dahlia blossoms should never be frozen for later use as dye.

Ingredients:

1 pound wool yarn, previously mordanted with alum
4 gallons dahlia blossoms
4 tablespoons tartaric acid
½ cup Glauber's salts

To make dye bath: Place four gallons of dahlia blossoms in a five gallon enamel container, cover them with water and boil for about forty-five minutes. Cool. Remove the refuse and the liquid becomes the dye bath.

To dye wool yarn: Add the wet, alum mordanted, wool yarn to the dye bath and simmer it for thirty minutes. Dissolve four tablespoons of tartaric acid and half a cup of Glauber's salts in one pint of hot water and add to the dye bath. Simmer the dye bath with the mixture for another thirty minutes. Cool. Rinse the yarn in warm water until the rinse is clear. Shake all the water from the yarn and hang it in the shade to dry.

Color: This recipe makes various shades of yellow and the color is fast. The dye bath may be used again for lighter shades.

Alternate fibers: Silk fibers dye well. Linen and cotton fibers do not respond well to this dye.

19. DANDELION BLOSSOMS WITH ALUM MORDANT

The dandelion blossoms should be cut as late in the season as they last. The more sunshine they have received, the stronger the dye substance. Only the flower heads should be used. Dandelion blossoms have to be used fresh; they cannot be frozen or dried.

Ingredients:

1 pound wool yarn, previously mordanted with alum
3 gallons dandelion blossoms
4 tablespoons tartaric acid
½ cup Glauber's salts

To make dye bath: Place the dandelion blossoms in a five gallon enamel container, cover them with about three and a half gallons of water and boil for about forty-five minutes. Cool. Remove the refuse and the liquid becomes the dye bath.

To dye wool yarn: Add the wet, alum mordanted, wool yarn to the dye bath and simmer for thirty minutes. Dissolve four tablespoons of tartaric acid and half a cup of Glauber's salts in one pint of hot water, add to the dye bath and simmer this mixture for another thirty minutes. Cool. Rinse the yarn in warm water until the rinse is clear. Shake water from the yarn and hang it in the shade to dry.

Color: This recipe makes various shades of soft yellow and the color is fast.

Alternate fibers: Silk fibers and soft spun cotton fibers dye well. Linen fibers do not dye.

20. DANDELION BLOSSOMS WITH TIN MORDANT

Cut the dandelion blossoms as late in the season as they last. The more sunshine the blossoms have received, the stronger the dye will be. Only the flower heads should be used. Dandelion blossoms cannot be frozen or dried; they must be used fresh.

Ingredients:

1 pound wool yarn, previously mordanted with tin
3 gallons dandelion blossoms
4 tablespoons tartaric acid
½ cup Glauber's salts

To make dye bath: Place the dandelion blossoms in a five gallon enamel container, cover with about three and a half gallons of water and boil for about forty-five minutes. Cool. Strain. The liquid is now the dye bath.

To dye wool yarn: Add the wet, tin mordanted, wool yarn to the dye bath and simmer for thirty minutes. Dissolve four tablespoons of tartaric acid and half a cup of Glauber's salts in one pint of hot water and add to the dye bath. Simmer another thirty minutes. Cool. Rinse the yarn in warm water until the rinse is clear. Shake water from the yarn and hang it in the shade to dry.

Color: This recipe makes various shades of yellow which are brighter in color than the shades produced when alum mordant is used. The color is fast.

Alternate fibers: Silk fibers dye well. Vegetable fibers dye lighter shades of color than the animal fibers.

21. DAY LILY BLOSSOMS WITH ALUM MORDANT

For dye purposes day lily blossoms should be cut when they are in full bloom. Different varieties may be combined as all varieties tested made yellow dyes with tin and alum mordants.

Ingredients:

1 pound wool yarn, previously mordanted with alum
4 gallons day lily blossoms
4 tablespoons tartaric acid
½ cup Glauber's salts

To make dye bath: Place four gallons of day lily blossoms in a five gallon enamel container, cover them with water and boil for about forty-five minutes. Cool. Remove the cooked blossoms and the liquid is now the dye bath.

To dye wool yarn: Add the wet, alum mordanted, wool yarn to the dye bath and simmer for thirty minutes. Dissolve four tablespoons of tartaric acid and half a cup of Glauber's salts in one pint of hot water, add this mixture to the dye bath, and simmer the bath another thirty minutes. Cool the yarn in the dye bath, then rinse it in warm water until the rinse is clear. Shake water from the yarn and hang it in the shade to dry.

Color: This recipe makes shades of yellow. The colors usually fade or soften a little.

Alternate fibers: Silk fibers dye well. Wool yarn that has metal spun with it dyes very well. This dye only produces very light shades when used on vegetable fibers.

22. DAY LILY BLOSSOMS WITH CHROME MORDANT

Cut day lily blossoms when they are in full bloom and use them within a few hours after cutting. The different varieties may be combined to make one dye bath.

Ingredients:

1 pound wool yarn, previously mordanted with chrome
4 gallons fresh day lily blossoms
4 tablespoons tartaric acid
½ cup Glauber's salts

To make dye bath: Place four gallons of fresh day lily blossoms in a five gallon enamel container, cover with water and boil for about forty-five minutes. Cool. Remove the cooked blossoms and the liquid becomes the dye bath.

To dye wool yarn: Add the wet, chrome mordanted, wool yarn to the dye bath and simmer for thirty minutes. The container should be kept covered when chrome is used. Dissolve four tablespoons of tartaric acid and half a cup of Glauber's salts in one pint of hot water and add to the dye bath. Simmer another thirty minutes, cool, then rinse yarn in warm water until rinse is clear. Shake water from the yarn and hang it in the shade to dry.

Color: This recipe makes a color range of gold and brass colors. The color fades very little, if at all. The dye bath may be used more than one time.

Alternate fibers: Silk fibers dye well. Vegetable fibers dye a color range of tan and brown colors.

23. DAY LILY BLOSSOMS WITH TIN MORDANT

The day lily blossoms should be cut when they are in full bloom for dye purposes. Different varieties may be combined to make one dye bath.

Ingredients:

1 pound wool yarn, previously mordanted with tin
4 gallons day lily blossoms
4 tablespoons tartaric acid
½ cup Glauber's salts

To make dye bath: Place four gallons of day lily blossoms in a five gallon enamel container, cover them with water and boil for about forty-five minutes. Cool. Remove the cooked blossoms and the liquid becomes the dye bath.

To dye wool yarn: Add the wet, tin mordanted, wool yarn to the dye bath and simmer for thirty minutes. Dissolve four tablespoons of tartaric acid and half a cup of Glauber's salts in one pint of hot water and add this mixture to the dye bath. Simmer another thirty minutes. Cool the yarn in the dye bath and then rinse it in warm water until the rinse is clear. Shake water from the yarn and hang it in the shade to dry.

Color: This recipe makes shades of yellow which are brighter than those produced when alum mordant is used. The colors will fade or soften a little from exposure to sunlight.

Alternate fibers: Silk fibers dye well. Vegetable fibers dye lighter than animal fibers.

24. FUSTIC WITH ALUM MORDANT

Fustic is one of the yellowwood tropical trees, and makes a good yellow dye. The chips are sold by commercial suppliers.

Ingredients:

1 pound wool yarn, previously mordanted with alum
1 pound fustic chips
4 tablespoons tartaric acid
½ cup Glauber's salts

To make the dye bath: Put the fustic chips into a cheesecloth bag, place in an enamel container, cover with two and a half gallons of warm water and soak for twelve hours. The chips should be loosely packed in the bag. After the bag of chips has been allowed to soak, boil it in the soaking water for about one hour. Press and squeeze the color from the bag several times while it is boiling. Cool. Remove the bag and the liquid becomes the dye bath.

To dye wool yarn: Add the wet, alum mordanted, wool yarn to the dye bath and simmer for thirty minutes. Dissolve four tablespoons of tartaric acid and half a cup of Glauber's salts in one pint of hot water and add this mixture to the dye bath. Simmer another thirty minutes. Cool. Rinse the yarn in warm water until the rinse is clear, and then squeeze the water from the yarn and hang it in the shade to dry.

Color: This recipe makes a strong bright yellow which is fast.

Alternate fibers: This recipe is good for all natural fibers except linen.

25. FUSTIC WITH CHROME MORDANT

Fustic will give a wide range of colors if different mordants are used with it. Chips from the trees are used for the dye, and these are sold by commercial suppliers.

Ingredients:

1 pound wool yarn, previously mordanted with chrome
1 pound fustic chips
4 tablespoons tartaric acid
½ cup Glauber's salts

To make dye bath: Put the fustic chips into a cheesecloth bag, place the bag in an enamel container, cover it with two and a half gallons of warm water and soak for twelve hours. The chips should fit loosely in the bag. After the bag of chips has been allowed to soak, boil it in the same water for about one hour. Press and squeeze the color from the bag several times while it is boiling. Cool. Remove the bag. The liquid is now the dye bath.

To dye wool yarn: Add the wet, chrome mordanted, wool yarn to the dye bath and simmer for thirty minutes. Dissolve four tablespoons of tartaric acid and half a cup of Glauber's salts in one pint of hot water and add this mixture to the dye bath. Simmer another thirty minutes. Cool. Rinse the yarn in warm water until the rinse is clear. Squeeze water from the yarn and hang it in the shade to dry.

Color: This recipe makes colors which range from golds to brasses. The shade will be determined by the amount of chrome that is used in the mordanting bath. The dye bath may be used more than one time for lighter shades of colors. It is fast.

Alternate fibers: This recipe is suitable for all natural fibers.

26. GOLDENROD BLOSSOMS WITH ALUM MORDANT

The goldenrod blossoms should be cut when they first reach full bloom, and should be used within a few hours after cutting. They cannot be frozen or dried for later use.

Ingredients:

1 pound wool yarn, previously mordanted with alum
4 gallons goldenrod blossoms
4 tablespoons tartaric acid
½ cup Glauber's salts

To make dye bath: Cut the goldenrod blossoms and that part of the stem nearest the blossom into 1" to 3" lengths, place in a five gallon enamel container, cover with water and boil for about two hours. The water may need to be replenished as it boils away. Cool. Remove the refuse. The liquid has now become the dye bath.

To dye wool yarn: Add the wet, alum mordanted, wool yarn to the dye bath and simmer for thirty minutes. Dissolve four tablespoons of tartaric acid and half a cup of Glauber's salts in one pint of hot water and add this mixture to the dye bath. Simmer another thirty minutes. Cool. Rinse the yarn in warm water until the rinse is clear. Shake water from the yarn and hang in the shade to dry.

Color: This recipe makes shades of yellow which are much softer than those produced when tin mordant is used. The dye bath may be used again for lighter shades. It is fast.

Alternate fibers: Silk fibers dye well. Linen and cotton dye very light yellow.

27. GOLDENROD BLOSSOMS WITH CHROME MORDANT

All of the goldenrod varieties tested for this book have produced good dyes. The shade of the color depends on the growing season, type of soil where the plant grows, and the variety of the plant. Goldenrod blossoms should be cut when they are first in full bloom, and they should be used within a few hours after cutting.

Ingredients:

1 pound of wool yarn, previously mordanted with chrome
4 gallons goldenrod blossoms
4 tablespoons tartaric acid
½ cup Glauber's salts

To make dye bath: Cut the goldenrod blossoms and that part of the stem nearest the blossoms into 1" to 3" lengths, place in a five gallon enamel container, cover with water and boil for two hours. The water may need to be replenished as it boils away. Cool. Remove the refuse. The liquid is now the dye bath.

To dye wool yarn: Add the wet, chrome mordanted, wool yarn to the dye bath and simmer for thirty minutes. Remember, the container should be kept covered when working with chrome mordanted fibers. Dissolve four tablespoons of tartaric acid and half a cup of Glauber's salts in one pint of hot water and add this mixture to the dye bath. Simmer another thirty minutes. Cool. Rinse the yarn in warm water until the rinse is clear. Shake the water from the yarn and hang it in the shade to dry.

Color: This recipe makes shades of gold and it is fast. The dye bath may be used again for lighter shades.

Alternate fibers: Silk fibers dye well. Linen and cotton fibers dye fairly well but the shades will be lighter.

28. GOLDENROD BLOSSOMS WITH TIN MORDANT

All of the varieties of goldenrod blossoms tested have produced good dyes. The shade of color depends on the growing season, type of soil where the plant grows, and the variety of goldenrod. The blossoms should be cut when they are well opened and ripe, but not brown or falling from the stems. Use the blossoms within a few hours after cutting.

Ingredients:

1 pound of wool yarn, previously mordanted with tin
4 gallons goldenrod blossoms
4 tablespoons tartaric acid
½ cup Glauber's salts

To make dye bath: Cut the goldenrod blossoms and that part of the stem nearest the blossoms into 1" to 3" lengths, place in a five gallon enamel container, cover with water and boil for about two hours. Cool. Remove the refuse and the liquid becomes the dye bath.

To dye wool yarn: Add the wet, tin mordanted, wool yarn to the dye bath, cover the container with a lid, and simmer for thirty minutes. Dissolve four tablespoons of tartaric acid and half a cup of Glauber's salts in one pint of hot water and add this mixture to the dye bath. Simmer another thirty minutes. Cool. Rinse the wool yarn in warm water until the rinse is clear. Shake out the water from the yarn and hang it in the shade to dry.

Color: This recipe makes a color ranging from bright yellow to gold. It is reasonably fast but should not be left in sunshine for extended periods of time.

Alternate fibers: Silk fibers dye well. Linen and cotton dye much lighter shades than wool and silk.

29. LILY OF THE VALLEY WITH TIN MORDANT

The lily of the valley plant is strongly affected by the growing season. In early spring it yields no color; in late spring and early summer it yields a yellow-green; in late summer and fall shades of gold and rust may be obtained from it. The stems and leaves are used to make the dye.

Ingredients:

1 pound of wool yarn, previously mordanted with tin
4 gallons lily of the valley stems and leaves
4 tablespoons tartaric acid
½ cup Glauber's salts

To make dye bath: Cut the lily of the valley stems and leaves into 1" to 3" lengths. Place them in a five gallon enamel container, cover with water, and boil for one hour. Cool. Remove refuse and the liquid becomes the dye bath.

To dye wool yarn: Add the wet, tin mordanted, wool yarn to the dye bath and simmer for thirty minutes. The yarn should be kept covered with liquid while the dye bath is simmering to prevent streaking. Dissolve four tablespoons of tartaric acid and half a cup of Glauber's salts in one pint of hot water and add this mixture to the dye bath. Simmer another thirty minutes. Cool. Rinse in warm water until the rinse is clear. Shake water from the yarn and hang it in the shade to dry.

Color: This recipe makes shades of yellow and gold. The dye bath may be used again to make lighter shades. It is fast.

Alternate fibers: Silk fibers dye very well. Linen and cotton fibers do not dye well.

30. MARIGOLD BLOSSOMS WITH ALUM MORDANT

The variety of the marigold blossoms will determine the shade produced, but all the varieties tested produced some shade of yellow or gold. Blossoms from different varieties of marigolds may be mixed, and blossoms from different flowers can be mixed, such as chrysanthemum blossoms and marigold blossoms. The blossoms can be dried in the sun, or in a slow oven, and used later. The blossoms should be picked when they are in full bloom.

Ingredients:

1 pound wool yarn, previously mordanted with alum
4 gallons marigold blossoms
4 tablespoons tartaric acid
½ cup Glauber's salts

To make dye bath: Place the marigold blossoms in a five gallon enamel container, cover them with water and boil for about forty-five minutes. Cool. Remove the refuse. The liquid is now the dye bath.

To dye wool yarn: Add the wet, alum mordanted, wool yarn to the dye bath and simmer for thirty minutes. Dissolve four tablespoons of tartaric acid and half a cup of Glauber's salts in one pint of hot water and add this mixture to the dye bath. Simmer the dye bath another thirty minutes. Cool. Rinse the yarn in warm water until the rinse is clear. Shake water from the yarn and hang it in the shade to dry.

Color: This recipe makes shades of yellow and it is fast. The dye bath may be used again to produce lighter shades.

Alternate fibers: Silk fibers dye well. Linen and cotton do not dye well.

31. MULLEIN WITH ALUM MORDANT

For dye purposes mullein should be cut in late summer, until the first frost. It can be used fresh or dry. The dry materials make a lighter color dye.

Ingredients:

1 pound wool yarn, previously mordanted with alum
4 gallons, cut up pieces mullein
4 tablespoons tartaric acid
½ cup Glauber's salts

To make dye bath: Cut the stalks and leaves of the mullein plant into 3" or 4" lengths, place them in a five gallon enamel container, cover with three and a half gallons water and soak for about twelve hours. After soaking, boil the mullein in the same water for about three hours. Enough extra water should be added to keep the materials covered during the boiling time. Cool. Remove the refuse and the liquid becomes the dye bath.

To dye wool yarn: Add wet, alum mordanted, wool yarn to the dye bath and simmer for thirty minutes. Dissolve four tablespoons of tartaric acid and half a cup of Glauber's salts in one pint of hot water and add this mixture to the dye bath. Simmer another thirty minutes. Allow the yarn to cool in the dye bath, and then rinse it in warm water until rinse is clear. Shake the water from the yarn and hang it in the shade to dry.

Color: This recipe makes shades of yellow and the color is fast.

Alternate fibers: The recipe is suitable for all natural fibers.

32. MULLEIN WITH CHROME MORDANT

Cut mullein for dye purposes during the late summer until the first frost. Mullein that has been cut in spring and early summer contains very little dye substance. Mullein cut for dyeing can be used fresh, or dry, but dry materials make a lighter color.

Ingredients:

1 pound wool yarn, previously mordanted with chrome
4 gallons cut up pieces mullein
4 tablespoons tartaric acid
½ cup Glauber's salts

To make dye bath: Cut the stalks and leaves of the mullein plant into 3" or 4" lengths, place them in a five gallon enamel container, cover with three and a half gallons of water and soak for twelve hours. Boil the mullein in the water in which it has been soaking for three hours. Enough extra water should be added to keep the materials covered with water while they are boiling. Cool. Remove refuse. The liquid is now the dye bath.

To dye wool yarn: Add the wet, chrome mordanted, wool yarn to the dye bath; simmer for thirty minutes. Dissolve four tablespoons of tartaric acid and half a cup of Glauber's salts in one pint of hot water and add this mixture to the dye bath. Simmer another thirty minutes. Remember, when working with chrome the container should be kept covered. Allow the yarn to cool in the dye bath, then rinse it in warm water until rinse is clear. Shake the water from the yarn and hang it in the shade to dry.

Color: This recipe makes shades of gold and it is a fast color.

Alternate fibers: All natural fibers respond well to this dye.

33. MULLEIN WITH TIN MORDANT

Mullein should be cut for dye purposes during the late summer until the first frost. Mullein that has been cut in spring and early summer contains very little dye substance. Mullein cut for dye purposes can be used fresh or dry, but dry materials will produce a lighter color.

Ingredients:

1 pound wool yarn, previously mordanted with tin
4 gallons cut up pieces mullein
4 tablespoons tartaric acid
½ cup Glauber's salts

To make dye bath: Cut the stalks and leaves of the mullein plant into 3" or 4" lengths, place them in a five gallon enamel container, cover with three and a half gallons of water and soak for twelve hours. Boil the mullein in the same water in which it has been soaked for three hours. Enough extra water should be added to keep the materials covered with water while the water is boiling. Cool. Remove refuse. The liquid is now the dye bath.

To dye wool yarn: Add the wet, tin mordanted, wool yarn to the dye bath; simmer for thirty minutes. Dissolve four tablespoons of tartaric acid and half a cup of Glauber's salts in one pint of hot water and add this mixture to the dye bath. Simmer another thirty minutes. Allow the yarn to cool in the dye bath, and rinse it in warm water until rinse is clear. Shake the water from the yarn and hang it in the shade to dry.

Color: This recipe makes various shades of yellow which are brighter than those produced with alum mordant. It is a fast color.

Alternate fibers: This recipe is suitable for all natural fibers.

34. PEACH LEAVES WITH ALUM MORDANT

Dyes can be made from peach leaves; the shade of color will be determined by the variety of the peach tree, the growing conditions during the season, and the time of season when they are picked. The best times to pick leaves for dye is during the late summer until the first frost. The leaves must be used fresh.

Ingredients:

1 pound wool yarn, previously mordanted with alum
4 gallons peach leaves
4 tablespoons tartaric acid
½ cup Glauber's salts

To make dye bath: Place the fresh peach leaves in a five gallon enamel container, cover them with water and boil for about two hours. Remove the cooked leaves and the liquid becomes the dye bath.

To dye wool yarn: Add the wet, tin mordanted, wool yarn to the dye bath and simmer for thirty minutes. Dissolve four tablespoons of tartaric acid and half a cup of Glauber's salts in one pint of hot water and add this mixture to the dye bath. Simmer another thirty minutes. Cool. Rinse the yarn in warm water until the rinse is clear, then shake the water from the yarn and hang it in the shade to dry.

Color: This recipe makes shades of yellow and it is a fast color. One dyeing usually exhausts the color so that it cannot be used again.

Alternate fibers: Silk dyes well. Vegetable fibers will dye a very pale yellow.

35. PEACH LEAVES WITH TIN MORDANT

The peach leaves should be picked during the late summer until the first frost for strong dyes. They should be used fresh.

Ingredients:

1 pound wool yarn, previously mordanted with tin
4 gallons fresh peach leaves
4 tablespoons tartaric acid
½ cup Glauber's salts

To make dye bath: Place the fresh peach leaves in a five gallon enamel container, cover them with water and boil for about two hours. Cool. Remove the leaves. The liquid has now become the dye bath.

To dye wool yarn: Add wet, tin mordanted, wool yarn to the dye bath and simmer for thirty minutes. Dissolve four tablespoons of tartaric acid and half a cup of Glauber's salts in one pint of hot water and add this mixture to the dye bath. Simmer the dye bath another thirty minutes. Cool. Rinse the yarn in warm water until the rinse is clear. Shake the water from the yarn and hang it in the shade to dry.

Color: This recipe makes shades of yellow which are brighter than those produced with alum mordant. It is a good base for top dyeing with a mild indigo solution to make bright greens. The dye bath can usually be used only once.

Alternate fibers: Silk fibers dye well. Vegetable fibers dye very pale.

36. QUEEN ANNE'S LACE WITH ALUM MORDANT

Queen Anne's lace is also known as wild carrot. This plant should be gathered when it is in bloom and the stems, leaves, and blossoms used for dye materials. They must be used fresh.

Ingredients:

1 pound silk yarn, previously mordanted with alum
4 gallons cut up pieces Queen Anne's lace
4 tablespoons tartaric acid
½ cup Glauber's salts

To make dye bath: Cut the whole plant, including the blossoms, into 3" or 4" lengths, place them in a five gallon enamel container, cover with water and boil for about two hours. Extra water should be added if it boils away. Cool. Remove the refuse. The liquid is now the dye bath.

To dye silk yarn: Add the wet, alum mordanted, silk yarn to the dye bath; simmer for thirty minutes. Dissolve four tablespoons of tartaric acid and half a cup of Glauber's salts in one pint of hot water and add to the dye bath. Simmer the dye bath another thirty minutes. Allow the yarn to cool in the dye bath, and then rinse it in warm water until the rinse is clear. Shake the water from the yarn and hang it in the shade to dry.

Color: This recipe makes a range of yellow colors. The colors are fast.

Alternate fibers: The recipe is suitable for all natural fiber yarns. Vegetable fibers dye lighter shades of color than animal fibers.

37. RED ONION SKINS WITH CHROME MORDANT

The onion is a versatile dye substance and the variety of the onion used in the dye bath will determine the color which is produced. Different varieties may be mixed when desired, or when it is necessary, but the results are unpredictable. The onion bulb will also make a dye.

Grocery stores and supermarkets are the usual sources of supply. They sometimes collect the skins when requested to do so, and some supermarkets have onion peeling machines and sell or give away the skins.

Ingredients:

1 pound wool yarn, previously mordanted with chrome
4 gallons dry red onion skins
4 tablespoons tartaric acid
½ cup Glauber's salts

To make dye bath: Place the four gallons of dry red onion skins in a five gallon enamel container, cover them with water and boil the water until the skins are almost clear. Cool. Remove the cooked skins. The liquid has now become the dye bath.

To dye wool yarn: Add the wet, chrome mordanted, wool yarn to the dye bath and simmer for thirty minutes. Remember to keep the container covered when working with chrome mordanted fibers. Dissolve four tablespoons of tartaric acid and half a cup of Glauber's salts in one pint of hot water and add to the dye bath. Simmer another thirty minutes. Cool. Rinse the yarn in warm water until the rinse is clear. Shake the water from the yarn and hang it in the shade to dry.

Color: This recipe makes dark gold and the color is fast. The dye bath may be used again to make lighter shades.

Alternate fibers: Silk fibers dye well and about the same shades as wool. Linen and cotton fibers dye to colors which range from tan to brown.

38. SAFFLOWER WITH COPPERAS MORDANT

Safflower powder can be purchased from commercial natural dye suppliers. The powder is made from the dried blossoms of the plant.

Ingredients:

1 pound wool yarn, previously mordanted with copperas
1 pound safflower powder
4 tablespoons tartaric acid
½ cup Glauber's salts

To make dye bath: Place the safflower powder in a lightweight cotton bag, about 12" square in size, tie the top, and place it in a five gallon enamel container. Cover the bag with three and a half gallons of warm water and soak it until all of the powder is wet. Boil for about two hours. Remove the bag of powder. The liquid is now the dye bath.

To dye wool yarn: Add the wet, copperas mordanted, wool yarn to the dye bath and simmer for thirty minutes. Dissolve four tablespoons of tartaric acid and half a cup of Glauber's salts in one pint of hot water and add this mixture to the dye bath. Simmer another thirty minutes. Cool. Rinse the yarn in warm water until the rinse is clear, and then shake the water from the yarn and hang it in the shade to dry.

Color: This recipe makes various shades of brass and the colors are fast. The dye bath may be used more than one time to produce lighter shades of color.

Alternate fibers: Silk dyes well. Linen and cotton dye lighter shades of color than silk and wool.

39. SEDGE WITH CHROME MORDANT

Sedge is a tall grasslike plant that usually grows in clumps in wet ground. The time to cut it for dye purposes is from spring until frost. The whole plant, except the roots, is used. It is a very fast dye.

Ingredients:

1 pound wool yarn, previously mordanted with chrome
4 gallons cut up sedge
4 tablespoons tartaric acid
½ cup Glauber's salts

To make dye bath: Cut the sedge into 6" to 12" lengths until there are about four gallons in quantity, place it in an enamel container and cover with about three and a half gallons of water. Boil for two hours. Replenish the water if it boils away. Cool. Remove the refuse and the liquid becomes the dye bath.

To dye wool yarn: Add the wet, chrome mordanted, wool yarn to the dye bath and simmer for thirty minutes. Remember to keep the container covered when working with chrome. Dissolve four tablespoons of tartaric acid and half a cup of Glauber's salts in one pint hot water and add this mixture to the dye bath. Simmer the bath another thirty minutes. Allow the yarn to cool in the dye bath, and then rinse it in warm water until the rinse is clear. Shake the water from the yarn and hang it in the shade to dry.

Color: This recipe makes shades of gold and the color is very fast. The dye bath may be used more than one time to produce lighter shades of color.

Alternate fibers: This recipe is suitable for all natural fibers.

40. TURMERIC WITH ALUM MORDANT

A dye can be made from turmeric in the form in which it is sold as a condiment, or in the packaged form sold by commercial suppliers especially for dyes.

Ingredients:

1 pound wool yarn, previously mordanted with alum
8 ounces turmeric
4 tablespoons tartaric acid
½ cup Glauber's salts

To make dye bath: Put the turmeric into a cheesecloth bag, place the bag in an enamel container, cover it with two and a half gallons of warm water and soak for twelve hours. The bag should be large enough to allow the turmeric to expand while it is soaking. After the turmeric has been soaked, boil the bag in the soaking water for about two hours. Press and squeeze the color from the bag several times while it is boiling. Cool. Remove the bag and the liquid becomes the dye bath.

To dye wool yarn: Add the wet, alum mordanted, wool yarn to the dye bath and simmer for thirty minutes. Dissolve four tablespoons of tartaric acid and half a cup of Glauber's salts in one pint of hot water and add to the dye bath. Simmer another thirty minutes. Cool. Rinse the yarn in warm water until the rinse is clear, then squeeze the water from the yarn and hang it in the shade to dry.

Color: This recipe makes yellow. The color fastness is fair to good.

Alternate fibers: Other natural fibers dye lighter shades of yellow than wool.

41. TURMERIC WITH CHROME MORDANT

A dye can be made from the turmeric which is sold as a condiment or from the form sold by commercial suppliers and packaged especially for dyes. The mordant determines the shade and sometimes changes the color.

Ingredients:

1 pound wool yarn, previously mordanted with chrome
8 ounces turmeric
4 tablespoons tartaric acid
½ cup Glauber's salts

To make dye bath: Put the turmeric into a cheesecloth bag, place it in an enamel container, cover with two and a half gallons of warm water and soak the bag for twelve hours. The bag should be large enough to allow the turmeric to expand while it is soaking. After the bag has been soaked, boil it in the soaking water for about two hours. Press and squeeze the color from the bag several times while it is boiling. Cool. Remove the bag and the liquid becomes the dye bath.

To dye wool yarn: Add the wet, chrome mordanted, wool yarn to the dye bath and simmer for thirty minutes. Dissolve four tablespoons of tartaric acid and half a cup of Glauber's salts in one pint of hot water and add this mixture to the dye bath. Simmer another thirty minutes. Cool the yarn in the dye bath, then rinse it in warm water until the rinse is clear. Squeeze the water from the yarn and hang it in the shade to dry.

Color: This recipe makes a color range of golds and brasses. It is fairly fast.

Alternate fibers: Natural fibers other than wool dye lighter shades of color.

42. YELLOW ONION SKINS WITH ALUM MORDANT

The variety of the onion will determine the color—yellow onion skins make yellow, red skins make shades of gold and rust. The onion bulb makes a lighter shade of yellow than its skins.

Grocery stores and supermarkets will often collect skins when requested to do so; some supermarkets have onion peeling machines and sell or give away the skins.

Ingredients:

1 pound wool yarn, previously mordanted with alum
4 gallons dry yellow onion skins
4 tablespoons tartaric acid
½ cup Glauber's salts

To make dye bath: Place four gallons of dry yellow onion skins in a five gallon enamel container, cover them with water and boil until the skins are clear. Cool. Remove the cooked skins and the liquid becomes the dye bath.

To dye wool yarn: Add the wet, alum mordanted, wool yarn to the dye bath and simmer for thirty minutes. Dissolve four tablespoons of tartaric acid and half a cup of Glauber's salts in one pint of hot water and add this mixture to the dye bath.

Simmer another thirty minutes. Cool. Rinse the yarn in warm water until the rinse is clear, then shake the water from the yarn and hang it in the shade to dry.

Color: This recipe makes shades of yellow and the color is fast. The dye bath may be used again to make lighter shades.

Alternate fibers: Silk fibers dye well and to about the same shades as wool. Linen and cotton do not dye well.

43. ZINNIA BLOSSOMS WITH ALUM MORDANT

Zinnia blossoms should be picked when they are in full bloom. The different varieties and colors may be mixed. All varieties and colors tested made shades of yellow when used with alum mordant.

Ingredients:

1 pound wool yarn, previously mordanted with alum
3 gallons zinnia blossoms
4 tablespoons tartaric acid
½ cup Glauber's salts

To make dye bath: Place the fresh zinnia blossoms in a five gallon enamel container, cover them with three gallons of water and boil for about thirty minutes. Cool. Remove the refuse. The liquid has now become the dye bath.

To dye wool yarn: Add the wet, alum mordanted, wool yarn to the dye bath and simmer for thirty minutes. Dissolve four tablespoons of tartaric acid and half a cup of Glauber's salts in one pint of hot water and add this mixture to the dye bath. Simmer another thirty minutes. Cool the yarn in the dye bath, then rinse it in warm water until the rinse is clear. Shake the water from the yarn and hang it in the shade to dry.

Color: This recipe makes a color range of yellows and the colors are fairly fast.

Alternate fibers: Silk dyes well. Vegetable fibers do not dye well.

V. Blues

Indigo is the best source of blue dye. It is also a good substance to use in top dyeing because the amount of the extract can easily be controlled by measuring—it is added to the water in measured amounts and tests with colored yarns can be made for desired shades.

Indigo works well as a top dye over yellow to make green, over red to make purple, and over brown to make black.

A few other plant parts will produce shades of blue.

44. ALKANET ROOTS WITH NO MORDANT

Alkanet roots exist in several varieties—some of them are known as henna roots, bloodroots, and puccoon. The variety of the alkanet roots and the mordant used with them will determine the color of the dye. The roots can be found in most areas and they can also be purchased from commercial sources.

Ingredients:

1 pound scoured wool yarn (no mordant)
½ pound dried alkanet roots

To make dye bath: Place the dried alkanet roots in an enamel container, cover them with two and a half gallons of warm water and soak for twelve hours. After the roots have been soaked, boil them gently in the same water for about two hours. Cool. Remove the refuse. The liquid is now the dye bath.

To dye wool yarn: Add the wet, scoured, wool yarn to the dye bath and simmer it for one hour. Cool. Rinse the yarn in warm water until the rinse is clear. Shake the water from the yarn and hang it in the shade to dry.

Color: This recipe makes shades of grayish blue and the color is fairly fast.

Alternate fibers: The dye is not suitable for fibers other than wool.

45. ELDERBERRIES WITH CHROME MORDANT

The purple-black elderberries were used for this recipe. They should be picked when completely ripe and used within a few hours.

Ingredients:

1 pound wool yarn, previously mordanted with chrome
4 gallons elderberries
4 tablespoons tartaric acid
½ cup Glauber's salts

To make dye bath: Cut the elderberries and their immediate stems into 1" to 3" lengths, place them in a five gallon enamel container, cover with water and boil for about one hour. Crush the berries while they are boiling and add more water if needed. Cool. Strain. The liquid becomes the dye bath.

To dye wool yarn: Add the wet, chrome mordanted, wool yarn to the dye bath and simmer for thirty minutes. Dissolve four tablespoons of tartaric acid and half a cup of Glauber's salts in one pint of hot water and add this mixture to the dye bath. Simmer another thirty minutes. Remember to keep the container covered when working with chrome mordanted fibers. Cool. Rinse the yarn in warm water until the rinse is clear. Shake the water from the yarn and hang it in the shade to dry.

Color: This recipe makes shades of greenish blue and the color is reasonably fast. The dye bath may be used again to produce lighter shades.

Alternate fibers: Silk fibers dye well. Linen and cotton dye very light colors and do not justify the effort.

46. HOW TO MAKE INDIGO EXTRACT, METHOD NO. 1

Indigo is the best natural source of blue dye. The plant can be grown in this country and powder made from the plant, for dye purposes, can be purchased from commercial suppliers of vegetable dyestuffs. The powder should be made from the parts of the plant which are above the ground and not the roots.

The indigo powder which is sold commercially is not soluble in water. However, sulfuric acid can be used to dissolve the indigo powder which in turn will make an indigo extract. The indigo extract can then be diluted with water to make a dye bath. The extract will remain in a usable condition almost indefinitely. This method of obtaining an indigo extract is less complicated and the extract is easier to use than the one that can be obtained by the vat method.

It is important that extreme caution be used when working with sulfuric acid. Do not breathe the fumes or allow the acid to come in contact with the body or clothing. Sulfuric acid burns can easily be lethal and it is deadly poison. It is wise to mix the extract outside when the air is still.

Ingredients:

4 ounces fresh, 100% strength, sulfuric acid
1 ounce indigo powder
½ ounce precipitated chalk

To make indigo extract with sulfuric acid: Slowly pour the sulfuric acid into a wide mouth glass bottle which has a screw on glass top, or stopper. Add the indigo powder to the sulfuric acid, a little at a time, and mix gently with a glass rod. Only a glass rod should be used for mixing; the acid will literally eat up wood or metal rods. The container becomes hot when the indigo is added to the acid, but if it is added slowly and a little at a time, then stirred gently, the container will not break.

Continue adding and gently mixing until the one ounce of indigo has been added. Screw on the glass top of the bottle and place the bottle in safe place in at least a 75° temperature for four days. The extract should be mixed once or twice a day during this time. The bottle may again become hot when the mixture is stirred, but with cautious stirring, it will not break.

At the end of four days, add half an ounce of precipitated chalk—the chalk can be purchased at most drug stores. Add the chalk a little at a time and mix it in gently. The mixture will again become hot and slowly spew while the chalk is being added. Do not allow the spewing particles to touch the body. Continue adding the chalk a little at a time and use a glass rod to stir the mixture after each addition, until the half ounce of chalk has been added. After the spewing stops, screw on the glass top and allow the mixture to set in at least a 75° temperature for another four days. During this time, the mixture should be stirred once each day.

The extract should be ready to use after eight days. If it is not, place the bottle in a warmer temperature, up to 85°, for two or three days longer. Time and temperature are important.

When the extract is ready it will be similar to a thin paste. Half an ounce of the indigo extract, added to two and a half gallons of water, will dye one pound of yarn to a medium shade of blue.

INDIGO (METHOD NO. 1) WITH ALUM MORDANT

This recipe is for dyeing with indigo extract made from sulfuric acid.

Ingredients:

1 pound wool yarn, previously mordanted with alum
½ ounce indigo extract
4 tablespoons tartaric acid
½ cup Glauber's salts

To make dye bath: Put two and a half gallons of warm water into an enamel container, add half an ounce of indigo extract and mix well. Always add the extract to the water. Heat the water until it is very warm to the touch and hold it at that temperature for five minutes. This is the dye bath.

To dye wool yarn: Add the wet, alum mordanted, wool yarn to the dye bath and simmer for twenty minutes. Dissolve four tablespoons of tartaric acid and half a cup of Glauber's salts in one pint of hot water and add this mixture to the dye bath. Simmer another twenty minutes. Cool. Rinse the yarn in warm water until the rinse is clear. Squeeze the water from the yarn and hang it in the shade to dry.

Color: This recipe makes a shade of medium blue. It is fast. To obtain darker or lighter shades increase or decrease the amound of indigo extract added to the dye bath.

Alternate fibers: This recipe is good for cotton and silk. Linen responds very poorly to this dye. Sisal, jute, and raffia dye well.

47. HOW TO MAKE INDIGO EXTRACT, METHOD NO. 2

A safe and simple method of dissolving indigo powder is with fermented human urine. It requires a minimum of two weeks to complete the process. This method can be used safely with groups involving children or other people who are untrained in handling dangerous chemicals.

Ingredients:

1 pint human urine
8 tablespoons indigo powder

To make indigo extract with human urine: Put the human urine in a tightly sealed glass jar and place the jar in the sunshine until the urine ferments. This will take about a week to ten days if the temperature is above 75° for several hours each day. When the urine ferments, the odor is very offensive and the liquid spews when the jar is unsealed. Eight tablespoons of powdered indigo should now be added, a little at a time, and stirred well into the urine after each addition. Allow the mixture to remain in the sunshine, or in a temperature above 75°, for another week to ten days. Stir or shake it well at least once each day. When the powder is dissolved, the liquid is the extract.

When the extract is diluted with water to make the dye bath, the odor is no more offensive than many other vegetable dye odors. One cup of this indigo extract added to two and a half gallons of water will dye one pound of yarn a medium shade of dull blue.

This extract is not satisfactory for top dyeing or mixing with other colors.

INDIGO (METHOD NO. 2) WITH ALUM MORDANT

This recipe is for dyeing with indigo extract made from human urine.

Ingredients:

1 pound wool yarn, previously mordanted with alum
1 cup indigo extract
4 tablespoons tartaric acid
½ cup Glauber's salts

To make dye bath: Put two and a half gallons of warm water into an enamel container, add one cup of indigo extract and mix well. Heat to very warm and hold there for about ten minutes. This is the dye bath.

To dye wool yarn: Add the wet, alum mordanted, wool yarn to the dye bath and simmer for thirty minutes. Dissolve four tablespoons of tartaric acid and half a cup of Glauber's salts in one pint of hot water and add this mixture to the dye bath. Simmer another thirty minutes. Cool. Rinse the yarn in warm water until the rinse is clear. Shake or squeeze the water from the yarn and hang it in the shade to dry.

Color: This recipe makes dull medium blue shades. It is fast. The amount of indigo extract used determines the shade and darker or lighter shades may be obtained by increasing or decreasing the amount of indigo extract added to the dye bath.

Alternate fibers: This recipe is suitable for cotton and silk. Linen fibers do not dye.

48. LOGWOOD WITH NO MORDANT

The dye is made from logwood chips and the chips can be purchased from commercial suppliers of vegetable dyestuffs. A variety of colors can be made from them.

Ingredients:

1 pound wool yarn
1 pound logwood chips
½ cup Glauber's salts

To make dye bath: Put the logwood chips in a cheesecloth bag, place the bag in an enamel container, cover it with two and a half gallons of warm water and soak for twelve hours. The chips should be packed loosely in the bag. After the bag has been allowed to soak, simmer it in the same water for one hour. Leave the bag in the water until the water is cool. Remove the bag. The liquid has now become the dye bath.

To dye wool yarn: Add the wet, unmordanted, wool yarn to the dye bath and simmer for thirty minutes. Dissolve half a cup of Glauber's salts in one pint of hot water and add this mixture to the dye bath. Simmer the bath another thirty minutes. Cool. Rinse the yarn in warm water until the rinse is clear, then squeeze the water from the yarn and hang it in the shade to dry.

Color: This recipe makes a range of blue colors. The dye bath can be used as long as it contains color, but the shades produced will be lighter each time the bath is used. The color is fairly fast.

Alternate fibers: This recipe will produce different shades on different fibers.

49. LOGWOOD WITH CHROME MORDANT

The dye is made from logwood chips and these can be purchased from commercial suppliers of vegetable dyestuffs. The wood comes from a tropical tree which grows in Central America and the West Indies. A variety of colors can be made from it by using different mordants.

Ingredients:

1 pound silk yarn, previously mordanted with chrome
½ pound logwood chips
4 tablespoons tartaric acid
½ cup Glauber's salts

To make dye bath: Put the logwood chips in a cheesecloth bag, place the bag in an enamel container, cover with two gallons of warm water and soak for twelve hours. The chips should be packed loosely in the bag. After the bag of logwood chips has been allowed to soak, boil it in the soaking water for about forty-five minutes. The logwood should be boiled longer if the pieces of wood are in chunks instead of small chips. Cool. Remove the bag. The liquid is now the dye bath.

To dye silk yarn: Add the wet, chrome mordanted, silk yarn to the dye bath and simmer for twenty minutes. Dissolve four tablespoons of tartaric acid and half a cup of Glauber's salts in one pint of hot water and add this mixture to the dye bath. Simmer another twenty minutes. Cool. Rinse the yarn in warm water until the rinse is clear. Squeeze the water from the yarn and hang it in the shade to dry.

Color: This recipe produces dark blue on silk fibers. The color is fast.

Alternate fibers: This recipe will make different colors on different fibers—for example, it makes black on wool fibers.

50. LOGWOOD WITH COPPERAS MORDANT

This dye is made from logwood chips which can be purchased from commercial suppliers of vegetable dyestuffs. The logwood tree is a tropical one, native to Central America and the West Indies. A variety of colors can be made from it by using different mordants and different fibers.

Ingredients:

1 pound wool yarn
3 ounces copperas
½ pound logwood chips
4 tablespoons tartaric acid
½ cup Glauber's salts

To make dye bath: Put the logwood chips in a cheesecloth bag, place the bag in an enamel container, cover it with two and a half gallons of warm water and soak for twelve hours. The chips should be packed loosely in the bag. After the bag has been allowed to soak, simmer it in the soaking water for one hour. Cool. Remove the bag. Add three ounces of copperas and dissolve it completely in the dye bath. This is the dye bath.

To dye wool yarn: Add the wet, unmordanted, wool yarn to the dye bath and simmer it for twenty minutes. Dissolve four tablespoons of tartaric acid and half a cup of Glauber's salts in one pint of hot water and add this mixture to the dye bath. Simmer another fifteen minutes. Cool. Rinse the yarn in warm water until the rinse is clear, then squeeze water from the yarn, and hang it in the shade to dry.

Color: This recipe produces a dark blue with gray tone. The color is fast. If four ounces of copperas is added and allowed to remain one hour in the dye bath, a black will be produced.

Alternate fibers: This recipe is suitable for all natural fibers.

VI. Oranges and Rusts

Yarns that have been dyed yellow can be top dyed with red in order to obtain orange and rust shades. Yellow and red dye baths can be combined. Raw materials, such as goldenrod blossoms and scarlet sage blossoms, can be cooked together to make orange and rust dye baths. Annatto, also, is a good source of orange and chrome mordant can often be used to make orange and rust out of a yellow dye material.

51. ANNATTO WITH ALUM MORDANT

The powdered annatto or annatto seeds used for this dye can be purchased from commercial natural dye suppliers. It is most commonly used for food and varnish coloring, but it makes a color that is rare among vegetable dyes—orange.

Ingredients:

1 pound wool yarn, previously mordanted with alum
½ pound powdered annatto
4 tablespoons tartaric acid
½ cup Glauber's salts

To make dye bath: Put the powdered annatto into a lightweight cotton bag, about 12" square in size, tie the top and place the bag in a five gallon enamel container. Cover the bag with three and a half gallons water and soak it until all of the powder is wet. After the bag has been allowed to soak, boil it in the soaking water for about one hour. The bag should be squeezed and pressed often while it is boiling to help release the color. Cool. Remove the bag of powder. The liquid is now the dye bath.

To dye wool yarn: Add the wet, alum mordanted, wool yarn to the dye bath; simmer for thirty minutes. Dissolve four tablespoons of tartaric acid and half a cup of Glauber's salts in one pint of hot water and add this mixture to the dye bath. Simmer another thirty minutes. Cool. Rinse the wool yarn in warm water until the rinse is clear, then shake the water from the yarn, and hang it in the shade to dry.

Color: This recipe produces an orange color and it is fairly fast. Although, sunlight may soften the color to some extent, it will not destroy it. The dye bath may be used more than once to produce lighter shades.

Alternate fibers: Silk fibers dye well. Cotton fibers dye lighter shades than silk and wool fibers.

52. BLOODROOT WITH NO MORDANT

The bloodroot plant can be found growing wild in many sections of the country and the fresh roots will make brighter dyes than dried ones. The dried roots can be purchased from commercial suppliers of vegetable dyestuffs.

Ingredients:

1 pound wool yarn
1 pound dried bloodroots
4 tablespoons tartaric acid
½ cup Glauber's salts

To make dye bath: Place the dried bloodroots in an enamel container, cover them with two and a half gallons of warm water and soak for twelve hours. After the bloodroots have been soaked, simmer them in the soaking water for two hours. Cool. Remove the refuse. The liquid is now the dye bath.

To dye wool yarn: Add the wet, scoured, wool yarn to the dye bath and simmer for thirty minutes. Dissolve four tablespoons of tartaric acid and half a cup of Glauber's salts in one pint of hot water and add this mixture to the dye bath. Simmer another thirty minutes. Cool. Rinse the wool yarn in warm water until the rinse is clear, then squeeze the water from the yarn, and hang it in the shade to dry.

Color: This recipe makes different shades of orange. The color is fairly fast.

Alternate fibers: Other natural fibers will dye to lighter shades than wool.

53. BLOODROOT WITH ALUM MORDANT

The bloodroot plant can be found growing wild in many sections of the country. When digging the roots, only a part of them should be taken from each plant so the plant will not be destroyed. The roots can also be purchased from commercial suppliers. They may be used fresh or dry.

Ingredients:

1 pound wool yarn, previously mordanted with alum
1 pound dried bloodroots
4 tablespoons tartaric acid
½ cup Glauber's salts

To make dye bath: Place the dried bloodroots in an enamel container, cover them with two and a half gallons of warm water and allow the dried bloodroots to soak for at least twelve hours. After soaking, simmer the bloodroots in the soaking water for about two hours. Cool. Remove the refuse. The liquid is now the dye bath.

To dye wool yarn: Add the wet, alum mordanted, wool yarn to the dye bath and simmer for thirty minutes. Dissolve four tablespoons of tartaric acid and half a cup of Glauber's salts in one pint of hot water and add this mixture to the dye bath. Simmer another twenty minutes. Cool. Rinse the wool yarn in warm water until the rinse is clear, then squeeze or shake the water from the yarn, and hang it in the shade to dry.

Color: This recipe makes colors that range from rust to orange, and the color is fast. The dye bath can be used again to produce lighter shades of color; the bath may also be used with different mordants but again the color will be lighter. The basic color will remain rust to orange, but different shades can be obtained by using chrome and tin mordants.

Alternate fibers: Linen does not dye well. Other natural fibers will dye to lighter shades than wool.

54. FUSTIC AND MADDER ROOTS WITH ALUM MORDANT

Orange can be made by dyeing a yarn that has been previously dyed yellow with a red dye. For example, orange can be obtained by dyeing a yarn with fustic the first time and then with madder the second time.

Ingredients:

1 pound wool yarn, previously mordanted with alum
1 pound fustic chips
½ pound madder roots
4 tablespoons tartaric acid
½ cup Glauber's salts

To make first dye bath: Put the fustic chips in a cheesecloth bag, place the bag in an enamel container, cover with two and a half gallons of warm water and soak for twelve hours. After the bag has been allowed to soak, boil it in the same water for one hour. Leave the bag in the water until the water is cool. Remove the bag. The liquid is now the first dye bath.

To dye wool yarn the first time: Add the wet, alum mordanted, wool yarn to the dye bath and simmer for forty-five minutes. Cool. Rinse the yarn in warm water until the rinse is clear. Squeeze the water from the yarn and hang it in the shade to dry.

To make second dye bath: Cut the madder roots into ½" lengths, place them in an enamel container, cover with two and a half gallons of warm water and soak for twelve hours. Simmer the roots in the water in which they have been allowed to soak for about forty-five minutes. Cool. Remove the refuse. The liquid is the second dye bath.

To dye wool yarn the second time: Wet the fustic dyed yarn in warm water, add it to the madder dye bath and simmer for fifteen minutes. Dissolve four tablespoons of tartaric acid and half a cup of Glauber's salts in one pint of hot water and add this mixture to the dye bath. Simmer the dye bath another fifteen minutes or until the desired shade is obtained. Cool. Rinse the yarn in warm water until the rinse is clear, then squeeze the water from the yarn, and hang it in the shade to dry.

Color: The recipe makes an orange color. The color is fast.

Alternate fibers: This recipe is suitable for all natural fibers. The shade of color varies somewhat depending on the fiber.

55. GUM CATECHU WITH NO MORDANT

Gum catechu (also known as cutch) is one of the best natural dyes. It does not grow in this country but it can be purchased from commercial suppliers.

Ingredients:

1 pound wool yarn
½ pound gum catechu
4 tablespoons tartaric acid
½ cup Glauber's salts

To make dye bath: Place the gum catechu in an enamel container and add two and a half gallons of very warm water. Stir the water with your hands until the gum catechu has dissolved. The substance is resin like and it becomes sticky and gummy when water is added so time must be allowed to dissolve it. This usually takes about thirty minutes of mixing and stirring. This is the dye bath.

To dye wool yarn: Add the wet, scoured, wool yarn to the dye bath and simmer for thirty minutes. Dissolve four tablespoons of tartaric acid and half a cup of Glauber's salts in one pint of hot water and add this mixture to the dye bath. Simmer another thirty minutes. Cool. Rinse the wool yarn in warm water until the rinse is clear. Squeeze or shake the water from the yarn and hang it in the shade to dry.

Color: This recipe makes colors which range from rusts to red-browns. The color is fast without using a mordant.

Alternate fibers: This dye is suitable for all natural fibers.

56. GUM CATECHU AND MADDER ROOTS WITH ALUM MORDANT

Rust, and a variety of shades of red-brown, can be made by dyeing yarns red that have been previously dyed medium brown or vice versa. An example would be yarn dyed a first time with gum catechu, and then dyed a second time with madder.

Ingredients:

1 pound wool yarn, previously mordanted with alum
½ pound gum catechu
½ pound madder roots
4 tablespoons tartaric acid
½ cup Glauber's salts

To make first dye bath: Place the gum catechu in an enamel container, add two and a half gallons of very warm water. Stir and mix the water with your hands until the gum catechu has dissolved. This is the first dye bath.

To dye wool yarn the first time: Add the wet, alum mordanted, wool yarn to the dye bath and simmer for forty-five minutes. Cool. Rinse the yarn in warm water until the rinse is clear, then squeeze the water from the yarn, and hang it in the shade to dry.

To make second dye bath: Cut the madder roots into ½" lengths, place them in an enamel container, cover with two and a half gallons of warm water and soak for twelve hours. Simmer the roots in the water in which they have been allowed to soak for about forty-five minutes. Leave the roots in the water until the water is cool. Remove the refuse and the liquid becomes the second dye bath.

To dye wool yarn the second time: Wet the gum catechu dyed yarn in warm water, add it to the second dye bath and simmer for fifteen minutes. Dissolve four tablespoons of tartaric acid and half a cup of Glauber's salts in one pint of hot water and add this mixture to the second dye bath. Simmer the bath another fifteen minutes. Cool. Rinse the yarn in warm water until the rinse is clear, then squeeze the water from the yarn, and hang it in the shade to dry.

Color: This recipe makes colors which range from rust to red-browns. The color is fast.

Alternate fibers: This recipe is suitable for other natural fibers, but they will dye lighter shades of color than wool. It is fast.

57. HENNA WITH TIN MORDANT

The powdered Egyptian henna sold by drug stores as a hair dye will also dye natural fiber yarns. Commercial natural dye companies also sell henna leaves for dyeing fabrics and yarns. Either form will make a good dye.

Ingredients:

1 pound wool yarn, previously mordanted with tin
½ pound powdered Egyptian henna
4 tablespoons tartaric acid
½ cup Glauber's salts

To make dye bath: Mix half a pound of powdered Egyptian henna with one quart of hot water and let it set for about one hour. Stir the mixture often to dissolve the powder, and then transfer it to a five gallon enamel container and add about three gallons of hot water. Mix well. This is the dye bath.

To dye wool yarn: Add the wet, tin mordanted, wool yarn to the dye bath and simmer for thirty minutes. Dissolve four tablespoons of tartaric acid and half a cup of Glauber's salts in one pint of hot water and add this mixture to the dye bath. Simmer another thirty minutes. Cool the yarn in the dye bath, and then rinse it in warm water until rinse is clear. Shake water from the yarn and hang it in the shade to dry.

Color: This recipe produces rust and rich red-brown colors. It is a fast color and the dye bath may be used more than one time. Of course, each time the dye bath is used, the color will be lighter.

Alternate fibers: Silk and mohair dye very well. Vegetable fibers will dye to lighter shades than animal fibers.

58. HOLLYHOCK BLOSSOMS WITH CHROME MORDANT

The different colors of hollyhock blossoms can be mixed to make one dye bath. The blossoms should be picked when they are in full bloom and used fresh.

Ingredients:

1 pound wool yarn, previously mordanted with chrome
3 gallons hollyhock blossoms
4 tablespoons tartaric acid
½ cup Glauber's salts

To make dye bath: Place the hollyhock blossoms in a five gallon enamel container, cover them with two and a half gallons of warm water and boil for about thirty minutes. Cool. Remove the refuse. The liquid is now the dye bath.

To dye wool yarn: Add the wet, chrome mordanted, wool yarn to the dye bath and simmer for thirty minutes. Dissolve four tablespoons of tartaric acid and half a cup of Glauber's salts in one pint of hot water and add this mixture to the dye bath. Simmer another thirty minutes. Cool. Rinse the yarn in warm water until the rinse is clear, then squeeze the water from the yarn, and hang it in the shade to dry.

Color: This recipe makes colors which range from orange to rust. It is fairly fast.

Alternate fibers: Vegetable fibers will dye to lighter shades than animal fibers.

59. LILY OF THE VALLEY WITH CHROME MORDANT

The lily of the valley will produce different colors, depending on the time of season when it is used. In early spring it has no color, in late spring it makes shades of yellow-green, and in the fall it makes shades of gold and rust. The leaves and stems of the plant are used to make dyes.

Ingredients:

1 pound wool yarn, previously mordanted with chrome
4 gallons fresh lily of the valley stems and leaves
4 tablespoons tartaric acid
½ cup Glauber's salts

To make dye bath: Cut lily of the valley stems and leaves into 1" to 3" lengths. Place them in a five gallon enamel container, cover them with water and boil for one hour. Cool. Remove the refuse and the liquid becomes the dye bath.

To dye wool yarn: Add the wet, chrome mordanted, wool yarn to the dye bath and simmer for thirty minutes. Remember to keep the container covered when working with chrome mordanted fibers. Dissolve four tablespoons of tartaric acid and half a cup of Glauber's salts in one pint of hot water, and add this mixture to the dye bath. Simmer another thirty minutes. Cool. Rinse the yarn in warm water until the rinse is clear, then shake the water from the yarn, and hang it in the shade to dry.

Color: This recipe makes different shades of rust and the color is fast. The dye bath may be used again for lighter shades.

Alternate fibers: Silk dyes very well. Linen and cotton dye fairly well.

60. MADDER (roots) WITH CHROME MORDANT

In this particular recipe madder roots were used, but the powder can be used with similar results. Madder roots can be purchased from commercial suppliers of natural dye materials.

Ingredients:

1 pound jute yarn, previously mordanted with chrome
1 pound madder roots
4 tablespoons tartaric acid
½ cup Glauber's salts

To make dye bath: Cut the madder roots into ¼" to ½" lengths, place them in a five gallon enamel container, cover with three and a half gallons of water and soak for about twelve hours. The roots will expand and absorb some of the water. After the roots have been soaked, add one gallon of water to the mixture and boil for about forty-five minutes. (Boiling brings out the yellow dye substance in the madder roots.) Cool. Remove the roots. The liquid is now the dye bath.

To dye jute yarn: Add the wet, chrome mordanted, jute yarn to the dye bath and boil it for thirty minutes or until the desired shade is obtained. (It is safe to boil jute fibers.) Dissolve four tablespoons of tartaric acid and half a cup of Glauber's salts in one pint of hot water and add this mixture to the dye bath. Simmer for thirty minutes or less, depending on the shade desired. Cool. Rinse the yarn in warm water until the rinse is clear, then wring or shake the water from the yarn, and hang it in the shade to dry.

Color: This recipe makes colors which range from orange to rust, and the color is fast. The dye bath may be used more than one time to produce lighter shades of color.

Alternate fibers: Linen and cotton fibers will dye in about the same way as jute. Silk and wool dye well.

61. MADDER AND SEDGE WITH ALUM MORDANT

This recipe involves combining two dye baths; the dye baths are made separately and then combined, in equal parts.

Ingredients:

1 pound wool yarn, previously mordanted with alum
½ pound madder roots
2 gallons cut up sedge
4 tablespoons tartaric acid
½ cup Glauber's salts

To make first half of dye bath: Cut the madder roots into ¼" to ½" lengths, place them in a three gallon enamel container, cover with two gallons of water and soak for twelve hours. During this time the roots will expand and absorb some of the water. After they have been allowed to soak, simmer the roots in soaking water for about forty-five minutes. Cool. Remove the roots. The liquid is the first half of the dye bath.

To make second half of dye bath: Cut about two gallons of sedge into 6" to 12" lengths and place in an enamel container. Cover the sedge with two gallons of water and boil for two hours. Cool. Remove the refuse. The liquid is the second half of the dye bath.

Combine the equal parts of the two dye baths (one and a half gallons of each). This is the completed dye bath.

To dye wool yarn: Add wet, alum mordanted, wool yarn to the dye bath and simmer for thirty minutes. Dissolve four tablespoons of tartaric acid and half a cup of Glauber's salts in one pint of hot water and add this mixture to the dye bath. Simmer another fifteen minutes. Cool. Rinse the yarn in warm water until the rinse is clear, then shake the water from yarn, and hang it in the shade to dry.

Color: This recipe makes different shades of rust and the color is fast.

Alternate fibers: The recipe is suitable for all natural fibers.

62. MADDER ROOTS AND YELLOW ONION SKINS WITH ALUM MORDANT

An orange color can be made by dyeing any strong yellow over yarns previously dyed a medium red or vice versa. For example, yarn can be dyed a first time with madder, and then a second time with yellow onion skins.

Ingredients:

1 pound wool yarn, previously mordanted with alum
½ pound madder roots
3 gallons dry yellow onion skins
4 tablespoons tartaric acid
½ cup Glauber's salts

To make first dye bath: Cut the madder roots into ½" lengths, place them in a five gallon enamel container, cover with two and a half gallons of warm water and soak for twelve hours. Simmer the roots in the water in which they have been allowed to soak for about forty-five minutes. Cool. Remove the refuse. The liquid is the first dye bath.

To dye wool yarn the first time: Add the wet, alum mordanted, wool yarn to the dye bath and simmer for thirty minutes. Cool. Rinse the yarn in warm water until the rinse is clear, then squeeze the water from the yarn, and hang it in the shade to dry.

To make second dye bath: Place the yellow onion skins in an enamel container, cover them with two and a half gallons of water and boil until the skins are clear. Cool. Remove the refuse. The liquid becomes the second dye bath.

To dye wool yarn the second time: Wet the madder dyed yarn in warm water, add it to the second dye bath and simmer for thirty minutes. Dissolve four tablespoons of tartaric acid and half a cup of Glauber's salts in one pint of hot water and add this mixture to the dye bath. Simmer another fifteen minutes. Cool. Rinse the yarn in warm water until the rinse is clear. Squeeze the water from the yarn and hang it in the shade to dry.

Color: This recipe makes an orange color and is fast.

Alternate fibers: Other natural fibers will dye lighter shades and these colors are fast.

63. POKEWEED BERRIES WITH CHROME MORDANT

Pokeweed berries should be picked late in the summer, after they have turned to a dark purple color. They can be used fresh or they can be dried and frozen for later use.

Ingredients:

1 pound wool yarn, previously mordanted with chrome
3 to 4 gallons pokeweed berries on stems
4 tablespoons tartaric acid
½ cup Glauber's salts

To make dye bath: Cut the pokeweed berries and stems into 1" to 3" lengths, place them in a five gallon enamel container, cover with water and boil for about forty-five minutes. If the berries are crushed while they are boiling, it will help to release the color from them. Cool. Remove the refuse. The liquid is now the dye bath.

To dye wool yarn: Add wet, chrome mordanted, wool yarn to the dye bath and simmer for thirty minutes. Dissolve four tablespoons of tartaric acid and half a cup of Glauber's salts in one pint of hot water and add this mixture to the dye bath. Simmer another thirty minutes. Cool. Rinse the yarn in warm water until the rinse is clear. Shake the water from the yarn and hang it in the shade to dry. After the yarn has dried, wet it again in warm water and return it to the same dye bath. Simmer for twenty minutes. Cool. Rinse. Dry. The second dyeing will practically eliminate fading.

Color: The recipe produces shades of rust and the color is fast.

Alternate fibers: This recipe can be used on all natural fibers.

64. POKEWEED BERRIES AND RED ONION SKINS WITH ALUM MORDANT

This recipe employs the top dyeing method in which a second dye is dyed on top of the first dye. It makes little or no difference which color is dyed first. The results obtained by top dyeing are similar to those obtained from mixing any two liquid dyes or dye substances which are compatible.

Ingredients:

1 pound of wool yarn, previously mordanted with alum
4 gallons red onion skins
4 gallons pokeweed berries

8 tablespoons tartaric acid
1 cup Glauber's salts

To make the first dye bath: Fill a five gallon enamel container nearly full of red onion skins, cover them with water and boil until the skins are almost clear. Cool. Remove the cooked onion skins. The liquid becomes the dye bath.

To dye wool yarn: Add wet, alum mordanted, wool yarn to the dye bath and simmer for about thirty minutes. Dissolve four tablespoons of tartaric acid and half a cup of Glauber's salts in one pint of hot water and add this mixture to the dye bath. Simmer for another thirty minutes. Cool. Rinse the yarn in warm water until the rinse is clear.

The wool yarn may be dried in the shade, or added immediately to the second dye bath. If it is dried before the second dyeing, wet the yarn thoroughly before adding it to the second dye bath.

To make second dye bath: Fill a five gallon enamel container nearly full with cut up pokeweed berries, cover the berries with water and boil for about an hour. Cool the berries in the water. Remove the refuse. The liquid becomes the second dye bath.

To top dye wool yarn: Add the wet, previously dyed, wool yarn to the pokeweed berries dye bath and simmer for about thirty minutes. Dissolve four tablespoons of tartaric acid and half a cup of Glauber's salts in one pint of hot water and add this mixture to the dye bath. Simmer another thirty minutes. Cool. Rinse the wool yarn in warm water until the rinse is clear, then shake the water from the yarn, and hang it in the shade to dry.

Color: This recipe makes various shades of rust and the color remains fast in water and sunlight.

Alternate fibers: Silk will dye well, but the dyeing time should be cut to half to prevent the silk fiber from disintegrating. Linen and cotton dye fairly well.

65. SAFFLOWER WITH TIN MORDANT

Safflower powder can be purchased from commercial natural dye suppliers. The powder is made from the dried blossoms of the plant and makes a good dye.

Ingredients:

1 pound wool yarn, previously mordanted with tin
1 pound safflower powder
4 tablespoons tartaric acid
½ cup Glauber's salts

To make dye bath: Place the safflower powder in a lightweight cotton bag, about 12" square in size. Tie the top and place it in a five gallon enamel container. Cover with three and a half gallons of warm water and soak until all of the powder is wet. Boil the bag of powder in the water in which it has been allowed to soak for about two hours. Cool. Remove the bag of powder and the liquid becomes the dye bath.

To dye wool yarn: Add the wet, tin mordanted, wool yarn to the dye bath and simmer for thirty minutes. Dissolve four tablespoons of tartaric acid and half a cup of Glauber's salts in one pint of hot water and add this mixture to the dye bath. Simmer another thirty minutes. Cool. Rinse the yarn in warm water until the rinse is clear, then shake water from the yarn, and hang it in the shade to dry.

Color: This recipe makes colors which range from rust to dark gold. It is a fast color. The dye bath may be used more than once to produce lighter shades.

Alternate fibers: Silk fibers dye well. Vegetable fibers dye lighter shades of color than animal fibers.

VII. Greens

Shades of dark green and yellow-green can be made from some plants by using blue vitriol or copperas as a mordant. Bright green shades are usually made by top dyeing or by mixing two dye baths.

66. BARBERRY PLANT WITH BLUE VITRIOL MORDANT

Any variety of the barberry plant will make a dye. It should be cut in late summer and fall for dyeing purposes, and it can be used fresh or dry.

Ingredients:

1 pound wool yarn, previously mordanted with blue vitriol
4 gallons cut up pieces barberry plant
4 tablespoons tartaric acid
½ cup Glauber's salts

To make dye bath: Cut the barberry canes and leaves into 3" or 4" lengths. The canes should be crushed before cutting to help release the color. Place the cut up pieces in an enamel container, cover them with three gallons of warm water and soak for twenty-four hours. After the barberry has been allowed to soak, boil it in the same water for two to three hours. Cool. Remove the refuse. The liquid is now the dye bath.

To dye wool yarn: Add the wet, blue vitriol mordanted, wool yarn to the dye bath and simmer for thirty minutes. Dissolve four tablespoons of tartaric acid and half a cup of Glauber's salts in one pint of hot water and add this mixture to the dye bath. Simmer another thirty minutes. Cool. Rinse the yarn in warm water until the rinse has become clear, then squeeze the water from the yarn and hang it in the shade to dry.

Color: This recipe makes a range of green colors. The shade will be determined largely by the time of season in which the plant is cut. It is a fast color.

Alternate fibers: This recipe is good for all natural fibers.

67. BARBERRY PLANT WITH COPPERAS MORDANT

The green and red leaf varieties of the barberry plant make good dyes and the color that results is very similar. The plant should be cut in late summer and fall, and it may be used fresh or dry. The dry plant will, however, produce a lighter color.

Ingredients:

1 pound wool yarn
4 ounces copperas crystal (ferrous sulfate)
4 gallons cut up pieces barberry plant
4 tablespoons tartaric acid
½ cup Glauber's salts

To make dye bath: Cut the barberry canes and leaves into 3" or 4" lengths and bruise or crush the canes to help release the color. Place them in a five gallon enamel container, cover with three and a half gallons of water and soak for twenty-four hours. After the barberry has been allowed to soak, boil it in the same water for three hours. Enough water to keep the materials covered should be added if it boils away. Cool. Remove the refuse. Add four ounces of copperas crystals (ferrous sulfate) to the liquid, and stir until they have completely dissolved. This is the dye bath.

To dye wool yarn: Add wet, wool yarn to the dye bath and simmer for thirty minutes. Dissolve four tablespoons of tartaric acid and half a cup of Glauber's salts in one pint of hot water and add this mixture to the dye bath. Simmer another thirty minutes. Keep the yarn covered with the liquid in the dye bath to prevent streaking. Allow the yarn to cool in the dye bath. Rinse the yarn in warm water until the rinse is clear. Shake the water from the yarn and hang it in the shade to dry.

Color: The recipe makes shades of dark green and the color is very fast.

Alternate fibers: This recipe is suitable for all natural fibers except silk.

68. BURLEY TOBACCO WITH BLUE VITRIOL MORDANT

Green burley tobacco leaves were used to make this dye bath. However, cured tobacco and some of the natural leaf twists of commercially packaged chewing tobacco may also give good results. Green tobacco should be used in late summer.

Ingredients:

1 pound wool yarn, previously mordanted with blue vitriol
2 pounds green burley tobacco leaves
4 tablespoons tartaric acid
½ cup Glauber's salts

To make dye bath: Cut the tobacco leaves into 4" to 6" length pieces, place them in a five gallon enamel container, cover with two and a half to three gallons of water and boil for about one hour. Cool. Remove refuse. The liquid is now the dye bath.

To dye wool yarn: Add wet blue vitriol mordanted, wool yarn to the dye bath and simmer for thirty minutes. Dissolve four tablespoons of tartaric acid and half a cup of Glauber's salts in one pint of hot water and add this mixture to the dye bath. Simmer another thirty minutes. Cool the yarn in the dye bath. Rinse the yarn in warm water until rinse is clear. Shake water from yarn; hang in shade to dry.

Color: This recipe makes shades of green with a brown tone and the color is fast.

Alternate fibers: Silk fibers dye well. Linen and cotton fibers dye lighter shades than wool and silk.

69. COCKLEBUR WITH COPPERAS MORDANT

All of the varieties of cockleburs tested for this book make very good natural dyes. They should be picked in late summer and can be used fresh or dry.

Ingredients:

1 pound wool yarn
4 ounces copperas crystals (ferrous sulfate)
4 gallons cockleburs
4 tablespoons tartaric acid
½ cup Glauber's salts

To make dye bath: Cut the cockleburs from the stalks, place them in a five gallon enamel container, cover with water and allow to soak for twelve hours. After they have been allowed to soak for twelve hours, boil the cockleburs in the same water for about two hours. Additional water may be needed to keep them covered while they are boiling. Cool. Remove the cooked cockleburs. Add four ounces of copperas crystals (ferrous sulfate) and stir them into the dye bath until they have completely dissolved. The liquid is now the dye bath.

To dye wool yarn: Add the wet, wool yarn to the dye bath and simmer for thirty minutes. Dissolve four tablespoons of tartaric acid and half a cup of Glauber's salts in one pint of hot water and add this mixture to the dye bath. Simmer another thirty minutes. The yarn should be kept covered with the dye bath to prevent streaking. Cool. Rinse the yarn in warm water until the rinse is clear. Shake the water from the yarn and hang it in the shade to dry.

Color: This recipe makes various shades of dark green and the color is fast.

Alternate fibers: No other fibers should be used. Do not use copperas on silk fibers. Linen and cotton will dye muddy gray.

70. FLORIBUNDA ROSE WITH COPPERAS MORDANT

Rose plants can be used to make dye; the plant need not be destroyed in order to obtain a dye from it. Trimmings from the plant should be cut in the fall, up until frost. The stems, canes, and leaves make the dye and these should be used fresh.

Ingredients:

1 pound wool yarn
4 ounces copperas crystals (ferrous sulfate)
4 gallons floribunda rose stems, canes, and leaves
4 tablespoons tartaric acid
½ cup Glauber's salts

To make dye bath: Cut the canes, stems, and leaves of the floribunda rose into 3" or 4" lengths, place them in a five gallon enamel container, cover with water and soak for about twelve hours. The stems and leaves should then be boiled in the soaking water for about two hours. Extra water can be added if it boils away. Cool. Remove the refuse. Add four ounces of copperas crystals (ferrous sulfate) to the liquid. Stir the copperas crystals into the liquid until they have completely dissolved. The liquid is now the dye bath.

To dye wool yarn: Add the wet, wool yarn to the dye bath and simmer for thirty minutes. Dissolve four tablespoons of tartaric acid and half a cup of Glauber's salts in one pint of hot water and add this mixture to the dye bath. Simmer another thirty minutes. Allow the yarn to cool in the dye bath. Rinse the yarn in warm water until the rinse is clear, then shake the water from the yarn, and hang it in the shade to dry.

Color: This recipe makes colors which range from dark green to black. The color is fast.

Alternate fibers: Copperas should not be used on silk fibers. The recipe is suitable for vegetable fibers but they dye lighter shades than wool.

71. FUSTIC WITH BLUE VITRIOL MORDANT

Fustic is a versatile dye when different mordants are used with it. It is one of the tropical yellowwood trees and chips for making dyes are sold by commercial suppliers.

Ingredients:

1 pound wool yarn, previously mordanted with blue vitriol
1 pound fustic chips
4 tablespoons tartaric acid
½ cup Glauber's salts

To make dye bath: Put the fustic chips into a cheesecloth bag, place the bag in an enamel container, cover with two and a half gallons of warm water and soak for twelve hours. The chips should be packed loosely in the bag. After the bag has been allowed to soak, boil it in the soaking water for about one hour. Press and squeeze the color from the bag several times while it is boiling. Cool. Remove the bag. The liquid is now the dye bath.

To dye wool yarn: Add the wet, blue vitriol mordanted, yarn to the dye bath and simmer for thirty minutes. Dissolve four tablespoons of tartaric acid and half a cup of Glauber's salts in one pint of hot water and add this mixture to the dye bath. Simmer another thirty minutes. Cool. Rinse the yarn in warm water until the rinse is clear. Squeeze the water from the yarn and hang it in the shade to dry.

Color: The recipe makes a green color and it is fast.

Alternate fibers: This recipe is suitable for all natural fibers. Linen will dye very light. The dye bath may be used more than once to produce lighter shades of color.

72. FUSTIC AND INDIGO WITH ALUM MORDANT

A variety of shades of green can be made by dyeing indigo over various yellow dyed yarns. An example is yarn that is dyed a first time with fustic, and then dyed a second time with indigo.

Ingredients:

1 pound wool yarn, previously mordanted with alum
1 pound fustic chips
indigo extract (amount is determined by the dyer)
4 tablespoons tartaric acid
½ cup Glauber's salts

To make first dye bath: Put the fustic chips into a cheesecloth bag, place the bag in an enamel container, cover with two and a half gallons of warm water and soak for twelve hours. After the bag has been allowed to soak, boil it in the soaking water for one hour. Cool. Remove the bag. The liquid is now the dye bath.

To dye wool yarn the first time: Add the wet, alum mordanted, wool yarn to the dye bath and simmer for forty-five minutes. Cool. Rinse the yarn in warm water until the rinse is clear. Squeeze the water from the yarn and hang it in the shade to dry.

To make second dye bath: Put two and a half gallons of warm water in an enamel container. Add the indigo extract a little at a time and mix it well into the water. Wet the fustic dyed yarn, then use small amounts of the yarn and test the color after each addition of indigo extract until the desired shade of green is obtained. The color in the test will be a little lighter than that of the simmered yarns. When the desired shade has been obtained, the liquid is ready for use as the dye bath.

To dye wool yarn the second time: Add the wet, fustic dyed, yarn to the dye bath and simmer for fifteen minutes. Dissolve four tablespoons of tartaric acid and half a cup of Glauber's salts in one pint of hot water and add this mixture to the dye bath. Simmer another fifteen minutes. Cool. Rinse the yarn in warm water until the rinse is clear. Squeeze the water from the yarn and hang it in the shade to dry.

Color: This recipe makes various shades of green. The shade will be determined by the amount of indigo extract in the second dye bath. The color is fast.

Alternate fibers: Linen is very difficult to dye, but other natural fibers dye well.

73. GOLDENROD BLOSSOMS WITH COPPERAS MORDANT

Goldenrod blossoms should be cut when they first reach full bloom. They should be used within a few hours after cutting.

Ingredients:

1 pound wool yarn
4 ounces copperas crystals (ferrous sulfate)
4 gallons goldenrod blossoms
4 tablespoons tartaric acid
½ cup Glauber's salts

To make dye bath: Cut goldenrod blossoms and the stems nearest the blossoms into 1" to 3" lengths. Place them in a five gallon enamel container, cover with water and boil for about two hours. Cool. Remove the cooked blossoms. Add four ounces of copperas crystals and stir until completely dissolved. The dye bath is now ready.

To dye wool yarn: Add the wet, wool yarn to the dye bath and simmer for thirty minutes. The yarn should be kept covered with the dye bath at all times to prevent streaking. Dissolve four tablespoons of tartaric acid and half a cup of Glauber's salts in one pint of hot water and add this mixture to the dye bath. Simmer another thirty minutes. Cool. Rinse the yarn in warm water until the rinse is clear. Shake the water out of the yarn and hang it in the shade to dry.

Color: This recipe makes shades of olive green and the color is fast.

Alternate fibers: Silk fibers dye well. Linen and cotton do not dye well.

74. GOLDENROD BLOSSOMS AND INDIGO EXTRACT WITH ALUM MORDANT

This recipe is made by combining two dyes; the yarn is first dyed yellow with goldenrod blossoms, then top dyed with indigo extract.

Ingredients:

1 pound wool yarn, previously mordanted with alum
4 gallons goldenrod blossoms
½ ounce indigo extract
4 tablespoons tartaric acid
½ cup Glauber's salts

To make first dye bath: Cut the goldenrod blossoms and the stems nearest the blossoms into 1" to 3" lengths, place them in a five gallon enamel container, cover with water and boil for about one and a half hours. The water should be replenished if it boils away. Cool. Remove refuse. The liquid is the yellow dye bath.

To dye wool yarn yellow: Add the wet, alum mordanted, wool yarn to the dye bath and simmer for thirty minutes. Dissolve four tablespoons of tartaric acid and half a cup of Glauber's salts in one pint of hot water and add this mixture to the dye bath. Simmer another thirty minutes. Cool. Rinse the wool yarn in warm water until rinse is clear, then shake the water from the yarn. The yarn can be dried and dyed later with indigo extract, or it can be dyed with indigo extract before drying.

To make second dye bath: Indigo extract should be made in quantity and kept on hand in a glass bottle with glass screw type top. To about two gallons of warm water, add about one fourth of an ounce of indigo extract and mix well. Use a small piece of yellow dyed yarn in the dye bath to test for the desired color of green. If the yarn does not appear dark enough, add remainder of indigo extract. Half an ounce of the extract will make fairly dark green. Remember, too, that wet yarns are darker than they are when they dry. When the yarn becomes the shade of color you want, the whole yarn can be dyed in the strength of indigo extract dye bath you have chosen.

To dye wool yarn the second time: Add the wet, yellow dyed, wool yarn to the indigo extract dye bath and simmer for about twenty minutes. Cool. Rinse the wool yarn in warm water until the rinse is clear. If the rinse does not clear, put the yarn back in the indigo dye bath, add one fourth of a cup of Glauber's salts and simmer another ten to fifteen minutes. With this method the color should not bleed but it does sometimes, and this is one way to stop it. Shake the water from the yarn and hang it in the shade to dry.

Color: This recipe makes a range of green colors, depending on the strength of both dye baths. It is fast.

Alternate fibers: Silk and cotton fibers dye well. Linen fibers are often difficult to dye.

75. GOLDENROD PLANT WITH COPPERAS MORDANT

The goldenrod plant contains dye substance and it makes a satisfactory dye when used with copperas for a mordant. It should be cut in the late summer or fall.

Ingredients:

1 pound wool yarn
4 ounces copperas crystals (ferrous sulfate)
4 gallons goldenrod plants (stalks and leaves)
4 tablespoons tartaric acid
½ cup Glauber's salts

To make dye bath: Cut the goldenrod stalks and leaves into 1" to 3" lengths, place them in a five gallon enamel container, cover with water, and boil for about two hours. The water may need to be replenished as it boils away. Cool. Remove the refuse and add four ounces of copperas (ferrous sulfate) and stir it until it is completely dissolved. This is the dye bath.

To dye wool yarn: Add the wet, wool yarn to the dye bath and simmer for thirty minutes. Dissolve four tablespoons of tartaric acid and half a cup of Glauber's salts in one pint of hot water and add this mixture to the dye bath. Keep the yarn covered with the dye bath to prevent streaking. Simmer another thirty minutes. Cool. Rinse in warm water until the rinse is clear. Shake the water from the yarn and hang it in the shade to dry.

Color: This recipe makes a dark green color and it is fast. The dye bath may be used again for lighter shades.

Alternate fibers: Copperas should not be used on silk fibers. Linen and cotton fibers will dye shades of dark greenish-gray. If some metal is spun with the vegetable fibers, they will dye very well.

76. GUM CATECHU (METHOD NO. 1) WITH BLUE VITRIOL MORDANT

Gum catechu is also known as cutch. It is a good dye and a very versatile one. It can be purchased from commercial suppliers.

Ingredients:

1 pound wool yarn, previously mordanted with blue vitriol
½ pound gum catechu
4 tablespoons tartaric acid
½ cup Glauber's salts

To make dye bath: Place the gum catechu in an enamel container and add two and a half gallons of very warm water. Stir the liquid with your hands until the gum catechu has dissolved. The resin-like substance becomes sticky and gummy when water is added, and it must be stirred and mixed for about thirty minutes before it dissolves. This is the dye bath.

To dye wool yarn: Add the wet, blue vitriol mordanted, wool yarn to the dye bath and simmer for thirty minutes. Dissolve four tablespoons of tartaric acid and half a cup of Glauber's salts in one pint of hot water and add this mixture to the dye bath. Simmer another thirty minutes. Cool. Rinse the yarn in warm water until the rinse is clear. Squeeze or shake water from the yarn and hang it in the shade to dry.

Color: This recipe makes a khaki color and is fast.

Alternate fibers: Other natural fibers do not dye this shade.

77. GUM CATECHU (METHOD NO. 2) WITH BLUE VITRIOL MORDANT

Gum catechu is also known as cutch. It is one of the best natural dyes and produces a number of different colors when different mordants are used. It can be purchased from commercial suppliers.

Ingredients:

1 pound wool yarn, previously mordanted with blue vitriol
½ pound gum catechu
4 tablespoons tartaric acid
½ cup Glauber's salts

To make dye bath: Place the gum catechu in an enamel container and add two and a half gallons of very warm water. Stir the liquid with your hands until the gum catechu is dissolved. The resin-like substance becomes sticky and gummy when water is added and must be stirred and mixed for about thirty minutes before it dissolves. This is the dye bath.

To dye wool yarn: Add the wet, blue vitriol mordanted, wool yarn to the dye bath and simmer for fifteen minutes. Dissolve four tablespoons of tartaric acid and half a cup of Glauber's salts in one pint of hot water and add this mixture to the dye bath. Simmer another fifteen minutes. Cool. Rinse the yarn in warm water until the rinse is clear, then squeeze the water from the yarn and hang it in the shade to dry.

Color: This recipe makes olive green and the color is fast. When the yarn simmers for a longer period of time the color becomes khaki.

Alternate fibers: This recipe is suitable for all natural fibers, but the shades of color will vary.

78. INDIGO WITH CHROME MORDANT

Indigo is an important vegetable dye because it is the best source of blue. It can be combined with yellow dyes or with chrome mordant to make green. The powder and lump forms can be purchased from commercial suppliers.

Ingredients:

1 pound wool yarn, previously mordanted with chrome
1 ounce indigo extract
4 tablespoons tartaric acid
½ cup Glauber's salts

To make dye bath: Add one ounce of indigo extract to three gallons of warm water in an enamel container. Mix well. Heat the mixture to very warm, 100° to 120°, and hold there for ten minutes. This is the dye bath.

To dye wool yarn: Add the wet, chrome mordanted, wool yarn to the dye bath and simmer for fifteen minutes. Dissolve four tablespoons of tartaric acid and half a cup of Glauber's salts in one pint of hot water and add this mixture to the dye bath. Simmer another thirty minutes. Cool. Rinse the yarn in warm water until the rinse is clear. If the dye rubs off on your hands while rinsing the yarn, put the yarn back in the same dye bath and simmer another ten minutes. Rinse again. Shake the water from the yarn, and hang it in the shade to dry.

Color: This recipe makes shades of green and the color is fast.

Alternate fibers: Cotton dyes well, but to lighter shades than wool. Silk will dye fairly well. Linen does not dye well.

79. INDIGO AND TURMERIC WITH ALUM MORDANT

A variety of shades of green, including bright green, can be made by dyeing indigo over various yellow dyed yarns. Yarn dyed a first time with turmeric then dyed a second time with indigo is an example.

Ingredients:

1 pound wool yarn, previously mordanted with alum
½ pound turmeric
indigo extract (the amount is determined by the dyer)
4 tablespoons tartaric acid
½ cup Glauber's salts

To make first dye bath: Put the turmeric into a cheesecloth bag, place the bag in an enamel container, cover with two and a half gallons of warm water and soak for twelve hours. The bag should be large enough to allow the turmeric to expand while it is soaking. After the turmeric has been allowed to soak, boil it in the soaking water for about two hours. Press and squeeze the color from the bag several times while it is boiling. Cool the bag in the water. Remove the bag. The liquid is now the first dye bath.

To dye wool yarn the first time: Add the wet, alum mordanted, wool yarn to the dye bath and simmer for forty-five minutes. Cool. Rinse the wool yarn in warm water until the rinse is clear. Squeeze the water from the yarn and hang it in the shade to dry.

To make second dye bath: Put two and a half gallons of warm water into an enamel container. Add indigo extract a little at a time, and mix it well into the water. Wet the turmeric dyed yarn. Use small amounts of the yarn and test the color obtained after each addition of indigo extract. Remember the test always appears a little lighter than the simmered yarns. When the yarn becomes the desired shade, the liquid is ready for use as the dye bath.

To dye wool yarn the second time: Add the wet, turmeric dyed, yarn to the dye bath and simmer for fifteen minutes. Dissolve four tablespoons of tartaric acid and half a cup of Glauber's salts in one pint of hot water and add this mixture to the dye bath. Simmer another fifteen minutes. Cool. Rinse the yarn in warm water until the rinse is clear. Squeeze the water from the yarn and hang it in the shade to dry.

Color: This recipe makes bright green and the color is fast.

Alternate fibers: Other natural fibers will dye lighter shades than wool. Linen is extremely difficult to dye and often does not take the color. The colors are fast on wool and other natural fibers.

80. LILY OF THE VALLEY WITH ALUM MORDANT

The color obtained from lily of the valley is largely determined by the time of the season when it is cut for use. If it is used in late spring, the color will be a yellow-green. Later in the season, the color changes to yellow, gold, and rust. The leaves and stems of the plant are used to make the dye bath.

Ingredients:

1 pound wool yarn, previously mordanted with alum
4 gallons fresh lily of the valley stems and leaves
4 tablespoons tartaric acid
½ cup Glauber's salts

To make dye bath: Cut lily of the valley stems and leaves into 1" to 3" lengths. Place them in a five gallon enamel container, cover with water and boil for one hour. Cool. Remove the refuse. The liquid is now the dye bath.

To dye wool yarn: Add the wet, alum mordanted, wool yarn to the dye bath and simmer for thirty minutes. Dissolve four tablespoons of tartaric acid and half a cup of Glauber's salts in one pint of hot water and add this mixture to the dye bath. Simmer another thirty minutes. Cool. Rinse the yarn in warm water until the rinse is clear. Shake the water from the yarn and hang it in the shade to dry.

Color: This recipe makes shades of yellow-green, more green than yellow. It is a fast color.

Alternate fibers: Silk fibers dye well. Vegetable fibers dye too pale to be considered a color.

81. PRIVET WITH BLUE VITRIOL MORDANT

Cuttings from a privet hedge can be used for making dyes if they are cut from midsummer until frost. The cuttings should be used while they are fresh.

Ingredients:

1 pound wool yarn, previously mordanted with blue vitriol
4 gallons cut up privet cuttings
4 tablespoons tartaric acid
½ cup Glauber's salts

To make dye bath: Cut the pieces of privet into 1" to 3" lengths, place them in an enamel container, cover with three gallons of warm water and soak for twelve hours. After the cuttings have been allowed to soak, boil them in the same water for about two hours. Cool. Remove the refuse. The liquid is now the dye bath.

To dye wool yarn: Add the wet, blue vitriol mordanted, wool yarn to the dye bath and simmer for thirty minutes. Dissolve four tablespoons of tartaric acid and half a cup of Glauber's salts in one pint of hot water and add this mixture to the dye bath. Simmer another thirty minutes. Cool. Rinse the yarn in warm water until the rinse is clear. Squeeze the water from the yarn and hang it in the shade to dry.

Color: The recipe makes a variety of shades of green. The shade will be largely determined by the time of the season when the plant is cut. The green is brighter than when copperas mordant is used.

Alternate fibers: This recipe is suitable for all natural fibers. The shade will vary with the fiber.

82. PRIVET WITH COPPERAS MORDANT

Cuttings from a privet hedge can be used for making dyes if they are cut between midsummer and frost. The cuttings should be used while they are fresh.

Ingredients:

1 pound wool yarn
3 ounces copperas crystals (ferrous sulfate)
4 gallons cut up privet cuttings
4 tablespoons tartaric acid
½ cup Glauber's salts

To make dye bath: Cut the pieces of privet into 1" to 3" lengths, place them in a five gallon enamel container, cover with three gallons of warm water and soak for twelve hours. After the cuttings have been allowed to soak, boil them in the same water for about two hours. Cool. Remove the refuse. Add three ounces of copperas to the liquid and dissolve it completely. This is the dye bath.

To dye wool yarn: Add the wet, wool yarn to the dye bath and simmer for thirty minutes. The yarn should be kept covered with the dye bath to prevent streaking. Dissolve four tablespoons of tartaric acid and half a cup of Glauber's salts in one pint of hot water and add this mixture to the dye bath. Simmer another thirty minutes. Cool. Rinse the yarn in warm water until the rinse is clear. Squeeze the water from the yarn and hang it in the shade to dry.

Color: This recipe makes a range of dark green colors. It is fast.

Alternate fibers: Vegetable fibers are likely to dye a muddy color. Silk does not dye well.

83. SEAWEED WITH COPPERAS MORDANT

The geographic location and the variety of the plant may have an effect on the colors obtained from seaweed. The seaweed for this particular dye was collected along the coast of Deer Isle, Maine, in July. The odor from boiling seaweed is pungent.

Ingredients:

1 pound wool yarn
4 ounces copperas crystals (ferrous sulfate)
4 gallons seaweed
4 tablespoons tartaric acid
½ cup Glauber's salts

To make dye bath: Place the seaweed in a five gallon enamel container, cover it with water and boil for about two hours. Extra water should be added as it boils away, and putting a cover on the container will help to reduce the pungent odor while the water is boiling. Cool. Remove the refuse. Add four ounces of copperas crystals (ferrous sulfate) to the liquid and stir it until completely dissolved. This is the dye bath.

To dye wool yarn: Add the wet, wool yarn to the dye bath and simmer for thirty minutes. The yarn should be kept covered with the dye bath to prevent streaking. Dissolve four tablespoons of tartaric acid and half a cup of Glauber's salts in one pint of hot water and add this mixture to the dye bath. Simmer another thirty minutes. Cool. Rinse the yarn in warm water until the rinse is clear. Shake the water from the yarn and hang it in the shade to dry.

Color: This recipe makes a dark yellow-green color. It is a fast color. If the dye bath is used more than once, the color may turn muddy.

Alternate fibers: Copperas should not be used on silk fibers. Linen and cotton dye muddy shades of greenish gray.

84. SEDGE WITH COPPERAS MORDANT

Sedge is a grasslike plant which usually grows in clumps in wet ground. It can be cut for dye purposes between spring and frost. The whole plant, except roots, is used. It is a very fast dye.

Ingredients:

1 pound wool yarn
4 ounces copperas crystals (ferrous sulfate)

4 gallons cut up sedge
4 tablespoons tartaric acid
½ cup Glauber's salts

To make dye bath: Cut the sedge into 6" to 12" lengths, enough to make about four gallons in quantity. Place in a five gallon enamel container, cover with three and a half gallons of water and boil for two hours. Enough extra water should be added to keep the materials covered while boiling. Cool. Remove refuse. Add four ounces of copperas crystals (ferrous sulfate) to the liquid. Stir until completely dissolved. This is the dye bath.

To dye wool yarn: Add the wet, wool yarn to the dye bath and simmer for thirty minutes. Dissolve four tablespoons of tartaric acid and half a cup of Glauber's salts in one pint of hot water and add this mixture to the dye bath. Simmer another thirty minutes. The yarn should be kept covered with the dye bath to prevent streaking. Allow the yarn to cool in the dye bath, then rinse it in warm water until rinse is clear. Shake the water from the yarn, and hang it in the shade to dry.

Color: This recipe makes dark gray-green and this is a fast color.

Alternate fibers: This recipe should not be used for silk. It is suitable for all other natural fibers.

85. SUMAC WITH BLUE VITRIOL MORDANT

The sumac, which has red berries, makes a good dye. The parts of the tree used for dye purposes should be cut late in the summer and fall, after the berries have turned red. They may be used fresh and they can also be dried for later use. The white berry variety should not be used; it is poison.

Ingredients:

1 pound wool yarn, previously mordanted with blue vitriol
4 gallons sumac berries, cut up twigs or leaves
4 tablespoons tartaric acid
½ cup Glauber's salts

To make dye bath: Cut the sumac into small pieces, put them into a five gallon enamel container, cover with three gallons of warm water and soak for twelve to twenty-four hours. After the sumac has been allowed to soak, boil it in the same water for two hours. Cool. Remove the refuse. The liquid is now the dye bath.

To dye wool yarn: Add the wet, blue vitriol mordanted, wool yarn to the dye bath and simmer for thirty minutes. Dissolve four tablespoons of tartaric acid and half a cup of Glauber's salts in one pint of hot water and add this mixture to the dye bath. Simmer another thirty minutes. Cool. Rinse the yarn in warm water until the rinse is clear. Squeeze the water from the yarn and hang it in the shade to dry.

Color: This recipe makes various shades of green and it is fast.

Alternate fibers: The recipe is good for all natural fibers.

86. SUNFLOWER SEEDS WITH BLUE VITRIOL MORDANT

The color that can be obtained from sunflower seeds depends on the mordant used with them. The mature dried seeds should be used.

Ingredients:

1 pound wool yarn, previously mordanted with blue vitriol
2 pounds dried sunflower seeds
4 tablespoons tartaric acid
½ cup Glauber's salts

To make dye bath: Place the sunflower seeds in an enamel container, cover them with three gallons of warm water and soak for twelve to twenty-four hours. After the seeds have been allowed to soak, boil them in the same water for two hours. Cool. Remove the seeds. The liquid becomes the dye bath.

To dye wool yarn: Add the wet, blue vitriol mordanted, wool yarn to the dye bath and simmer for thirty minutes. Dissolve four tablespoons of tartaric acid and half a cup of Glauber's salts in one pint of hot water and add this mixture to the dye bath. Simmer another thirty minutes. Cool. Rinse the yarn until the rinse is clear in warm water. Shake the water from the yarn and hang it in the shade to dry.

Color: This recipe makes various shades of green on wool and the color is fast.

Alternate fibers: The recipe produces gray on silk. Vegetable fibers do not dye.

87. TURMERIC WITH BLUE VITRIOL MORDANT

A dye can be made from the turmeric which is sold as a condiment, or from the form sold by commercial suppliers and packaged especially for dyes.

Ingredients:

1 pound wool yarn, previously mordanted with blue vitriol
8 ounces turmeric
4 tablespoons tartaric acid
½ cup Glauber's salts

To make dye bath: Put the turmeric into a cheesecloth bag, place the bag in an enamel container, cover with two and a half gallons of warm water and soak for twelve hours. The bag should be large enough to allow the turmeric to expand while it is soaking. After the turmeric has been allowed to soak, boil it in the soaking water for about two hours. Press and squeeze the color from the bag several times while it is boiling. Cool. Remove the bag. The liquid is now the dye bath.

To dye wool yarn: Add the wet, blue vitriol mordanted, wool yarn to the dye bath and simmer for thirty minutes. Dissolve four tablespoons of tartaric acid and half a cup of Glauber's salts in one pint of hot water and add this mixture to the dye bath. Simmer another thirty minutes. Cool the yarn in the dye bath. Rinse yarn in warm water until rinse is clear. Squeeze water from yarn and hang in shade to dry.

Color: This recipe makes a green color and it is fairly fast.

Alternate fibers: Other natural fibers dye lighter shades of color than wool.

VIII. Lavenders and Purples

Lavender and purple dye materials are fairly easy to find. Some varieties of grapes, berries, plums, and blossoms make a purple dye. These colors can also be obtained by top dyeing blue over red, or red over blue, or by mixing a red dye bath with a blue one. In the top dyeing method, it seems easier to dye blue over red.

The lavender color is usually a light shade of purple, and a purple dye bath, diluted with water, will make lavender. Other materials, such as mulberry, produce a lavender color which is as dark as the dye will be.

Mordants are often a determining factor in making purple.

88. ALKANET ROOTS WITH NO MORDANT

Alkanet roots can be purchased from commercial suppliers and the variety of the plant, as well as the mordant, will determine the color.

Ingredients:

1 pound wool yarn
½ pound alkanet roots
1 cup 36% acetic acid
½ cup Glauber's salts

To make dye bath: Place the dried alkanet roots in an enamel container, cover them with two and a half gallons of warm water and soak for twelve hours. After the roots have been allowed to soak, boil them in the same water for about two hours. Cool. Remove refuse. Add one cup 36% acetic acid; mix. This is the dye bath.

To dye wool yarn: Add the wet, scoured, wool yarn to the dye bath and simmer for thirty minutes. Dissolve half a cup of Glauber's salts in one pint of hot water and add this mixture to the dye bath. Simmer another thirty minutes. Cool. Rinse the yarn in warm water until the rinse is clear. Squeeze or shake water from the yarn, and hang it in the shade to dry.

Color: This recipe makes a reddish-purple color with brown tones. It is fast.

Alternate fibers: This is not a very good dye for other fibers.

89. BLACKBERRIES WITH ALUM MORDANT

A dye bath can be made from fresh or frozen blackberries. The blackberries should be picked when they are absolutely ripe.

Ingredients:

1 pound wool yarn, previously mordanted with alum
2 gallons fresh or frozen ripe blackberries
4 tablespoons tartaric acid
½ cup Glauber's salts

To make dye bath: Place the two gallons of blackberries in a five gallon enamel container and cover them with three and a half gallons of water. Boil the blackberries for about one hour, or until the color has been boiled out of the berries. The berries should be crushed while they are boiling to obtain all of the color. Cool. Strain. The liquid is the dye bath.

To dye wool yarn: Add the wet, alum mordanted, wool yarn to the dye bath; simmer for thirty minutes. Dissolve four tablespoons of tartaric acid and half a cup of Glauber's salts in one pint of hot water, and add this mixture to the dye bath. Simmer another thirty minutes. Cool. Rinse the yarn in warm water until the rinse is clear. Shake the water from the yarn and hang it in the shade to dry.

Color: This recipe makes a purple which often has a brown tone. The color will fade in the sunlight, but it will not lose color completely. The dye bath may be used more than once to produce lighter shades.

Alternate fibers: Silk fibers dye about the same shades of color as wool. Linen and cotton dye lighter in color.

90. BLACKBERRIES WITH TIN MORDANT

The wild or cultivated varieties of blackberries will make a dye when they are ripe. They can be used fresh or they can be frozen for later use.

Ingredients:

1 pound wool yarn, previously mordanted with tin
2 gallons fresh or frozen ripe blackberries
4 tablespoons tartaric acid
½ cup Glauber's salts

To make dye bath: Place the two gallons of ripe blackberries in a five gallon enamel container and cover them with three and a half gallons of water. Boil the blackberries for about one hour, or until the color has been boiled out of the berries. The berries should be crushed while they are boiling to release all of the color. Cool. Strain. The liquid is the dye bath.

To dye wool yarn: Add the wet, tin mordanted, wool yarn to the dye bath; simmer for thirty minutes. Dissolve four tablespoons of tartaric acid and half a cup of Glauber's salts in one pint of hot water and add this mixture to the dye bath. Simmer another thirty minutes. Cool. Rinse the wool yarn in warm water until the rinse is clear, then shake the water from yarn, and hang it in the shade to dry.

Color: This recipe makes various shades of bright purple. The color will fade a little but it will not lose color entirely. The dye bath may be used more than once to obtain lighter shades of purple.

Alternate fibers: Silk, linen, and cotton fibers dye well.

91. COCHINEAL WITH CHROME MORDANT

Cochineal is an excellent natural dye substance. It can be purchased in powder form from natural dye supply companies. If different mordants are used with it, shades of red, purple, and black can be obtained.

Ingredients:

1 pound of wool yarn, previously mordanted with chrome
½ pound powdered cochineal
4 tablespoons tartaric acid
½ cup Glauber's salts

To make dye bath: Mix the cochineal powder with enough warm water to make a thin paste. Use a one gallon glass or enamel container to allow for the thickening and expansion of the mixture. Allow the mixture to stand for about twelve hours and stir it three or four times during this time. After the mixture has been allowed to stand, transfer it into a five gallon enamel container and add three gallons of warm water. Add the water slowly and stir at the same time to dissolve the lumps and thick masses of powder in the original mixture. Heat to simmer and hold it at that temperature for about ten minutes. This is the dye bath.

To dye wool yarn: Add the wet, chrome mordanted, wool yarn to the dye bath and simmer it for about thirty minutes. Dissolve four tablespoons of tartaric acid and half a cup of Glauber's salts in one pint of hot water and add this mixture to the dye bath. Simmer for another thirty minutes. Cool. Rinse the yarn in warm water until the rinse is clear, then shake out the water and hang it in the shade to dry.

Color: This recipe makes a purple color and it is fast. The dye bath can be used over again until the color is gone. Each successive dyeing will produce a lighter shade.

Alternate fibers: Silk fibers dye well.

92. COCHINEAL AND INDIGO WITH ALUM MORDANT

A variety of shades of purple and lavender can be made by using an indigo dye over yarns previously dyed red. The blue-reds or a true red must be used, since yellow-reds dyed with indigo will produce browns and shades of greens. If yarn is dyed a first time with crimson cochineal, and then dyed a second time with indigo, it will be purple in color.

Ingredients:

1 pound wool yarn, previously mordanted with alum
½ pound crimson cochineal powder
indigo extract (the amount is determined by the dyer)
4 tablespoons tartaric acid
½ cup Glauber's salts

To make first dye bath: Mix the cochineal powder with enough warm water to make a thin paste, and allow the mixture to set for twelve hours. The container should be large enough to allow for expansion. After twelve hours, transfer the mixture to an enamel container and add two and a half gallons of warm water. Mix the liquid well with your hands and dissolve all the lumps. Heat to simmer and hold there for ten minutes. This is the first dye bath.

To dye wool yarn the first time: Add the wet, alum mordanted, wool yarn to the dye bath and simmer it for thirty minutes. Cool. Rinse the yarn in warm water until the rinse is clear. Squeeze the water from the yarn and hang it in the shade to dry.

To make second dye bath: Put two and a half gallons of warm water into an enamel container. Add indigo extract a little at a time. Mix the extract well into the liquid. Wet cochineal dyed yarn. Use small amounts of the yarn to test the color after each addition of indigo extract is added until desired shade of purple is obtained. Remember, the test will be a little lighter than the simmered yarns. When the desired shade is obtained, the liquid is the second dye bath.

To dye wool yarn the second time: Add the wet, cochineal dyed, yarn to the dye bath and simmer for fifteen minutes. Dissolve four tablespoons of tartaric acid and half a cup of Glauber's salts in one pint of hot water and add this mixture to the dye bath. Simmer another fifteen minutes. Cool. Rinse the yarn in warm water until the rinse is clear. Squeeze the water from the yarn and hang it in the shade to dry.

Color: This recipe makes a purple color and it is fast.

Alternate fibers: Other natural fibers dye lighter shades than wool. Linen dyes very poorly.

93. COCHINEAL AND MADDER WITH ALUM MORDANT

This recipe combines two dye baths. The dye baths are made separately then combined, in equal parts, to make one dye bath.

Ingredients:

1 pound wool yarn, previously mordanted with alum
½ pound powdered cochineal
½ pound madder roots
4 tablespoons tartaric acid
½ cup Glauber's salts

To make first half of dye bath: Mix the cochineal powder with enough water to make a thin paste. A larger container should be used than that which appears necessary, because the mixture will expand and become thick. The mixture should be allowed to set for about twelve hours and stirred three or four times during that time. After the mixture has set, transfer the mixture to a large enamel container and add two gallons of warm water. Add the water slowly and stir to dissolve lumps and thick masses of powder. This is the first half of the dye bath.

To make second half of the dye bath: Cut the madder roots into ¼" to ½" lengths, place them in a three gallon enamel container, cover with two gallons of water and soak for twelve hours. The roots will expand and absorb some of the water. After they have been allowed to soak, simmer the roots in the same water for about forty-five minutes. Cool. Remove the roots and the liquid is the second half of the dye bath. Pour one and a half gallons of each liquid into a five gallon enamel container and heat to simmer for fifteen minutes. The liquid has now become dye bath.

To dye wool yarn: Add the wet, alum mordanted, wool yarn to the dye bath; simmer for thirty minutes. Dissolve four tablespoons of tartaric acid and half a cup of Glauber's salts in one pint hot water and add this mixture to the dye bath. Simmer another fifteen minutes. Allow the yarn to cool in the dye bath. Rinse in warm water until rinse is clear. Shake the water from the yarn and hang it in the shade to dry.

Color: This recipe makes various shades of purple that have a brown tone; the color is fast. The dye bath may be used more than once to produce lighter shades.

Alternate fibers: The recipe is suitable for all natural fibers. Vegetable fibers will dye lighter shades than animal fibers.

94. CONCORD GRAPES WITH ALUM MORDANT

The purple grape, known as Concord, contains dye substance when it is ripe. It should be used fresh.

Ingredients:

1 pound wool yarn, previously mordanted with alum
3 gallons Concord grapes picked from stems
4 tablespoons tartaric acid
½ cup Glauber's salts

To make dye bath: Pick three gallons of Concord grapes from their stems, place them in a five gallon enamel container and cover with about three and a half gallons of water. Boil them for about one hour or until color has boiled out of the grapes. Crush the grapes while boiling to help remove the color. Cool. Strain. The liquid is the dye bath.

To dye wool yarn: Add the wet, alum mordanted, wool yarn to the dye bath; simmer for thirty minutes. Dissolve four tablespoons of tartaric acid and half a cup of Glauber's salts in one pint of hot water and add this mixture to the dye bath. Simmer another thirty minutes. Cool yarn in the dye bath. Rinse in warm water until the rinse has become clear. Shake the water from the yarn and hang in in the shade to dry.

Color: The recipe makes a color range of lavenders and purples; the colors often have a brown tone. It is fairly fast.

Alternate fibers: This recipe is suitable for all natural fibers.

95. CONCORD GRAPES WITH TIN MORDANT

The purple grape, known as Concord, contains dye substance when it is ripe. It should be used fresh.

Ingredients:

1 pound wool yarn, previously mordanted with tin
3 gallons Concord grapes picked from stems
4 tablespoons tartaric acid
½ cup Glauber's salts

To make dye bath: Pick three gallons of Concord grapes from their stems, place them in a five gallon enamel container and cover with about three and a half gallons of water. Boil for about an hour or until color has boiled out of the grapes. Crush the grapes while they are boiling to help remove the color. Cool. Strain. The liquid is the dye bath.

To dye wool yarn: Add the wet, tin mordanted, wool yarn to the dye bath; simmer for thirty minutes. Dissolve four tablespoons of tartaric acid and half a cup of Glauber's salts in one pint of hot water and add this mixture to the dye bath. Simmer another thirty minutes. Cool the yarn in the dye bath, then rinse it in warm water until rinse is clear. Shake the water from the yarn and hang it in the shade to dry.

Color: The recipe makes various shades of purple. The color is brighter than that obtained when alum mordant is used. It is fairly fast.

Alternate fibers: This recipe is suitable for all natural fibers.

96. CUDBEAR WITH TIN MORDANT

Cudbear can be purchased from commercial suppliers. The powdered dyestuff is made from lichens.

Ingredients:

1 pound of wool yarn, previously mordanted with tin
4 ounces powdered cudbear
4 tablespoons tartaric acid
½ cup Glauber's salts

To make dye bath: Mix four ounces of cudbear with one quart of warm water in a glass or an enamel container. Stir and mix the water until the powder has completely dissolved; it will then be a thin paste. Put three gallons of warm water in an enamel container and add it to the mixture a little at a time. Stir the liquid with your hand and rub any remaining lumps of powder between your fingers to dissolve them. Heat to simmer and hold the mixture at that temperature for fifteen minutes. Stir it again thoroughly. This is the dye bath.

To dye wool yarn: Add the wet, tin mordanted, wool yarn to the dye bath and simmer for twenty minutes. Dissolve four tablespoons of tartaric acid and half a cup of Glauber's salts in one pint of hot water and add this mixture to the dye bath. Simmer it another twenty minutes. Cool. Rinse the yarn in warm water until the rinse is clear. Shake the water from the yarn and hang it in the shade to dry.

Color: This recipe makes a color range of purples and the color is fast. The dye bath can be used three or four times to produce lighter shades, such as violet and lavender.

Alternate fibers: This is a good dyestuff for all natural fibers. Linen, cotton, and silk dye lighter shades than wool.

97. ELDERBERRIES WITH ALUM MORDANT

The purple-black elderberries were used in this recipe. They should be picked when completely ripe, and used within a few hours after they have been picked. The berries can also be frozen for later use.

Ingredients:

1 pound wool yarn, previously mordanted with alum
4 gallons elderberries
4 tablespoons tartaric acid
½ cup Glauber's salts

To make dye bath: Cut the elderberries and the part of the stem nearest the berry into 1" to 3" lengths. Place them in a five gallon enamel container, cover with water and boil for about one hour. The berries should be crushed while they are boiling and enough water should be added to keep the berries covered with liquid. Cool. Strain. The liquid becomes the dye bath.

To dye wool yarn: Add the wet, alum mordanted, wool yarn to the dye bath and simmer for thirty minutes. Dissolve four tablespoons of tartaric acid and half a cup of Glauber's salts in one pint of hot water and add this mixture to the dye bath. Simmer another thirty minutes. Cool. Rinse the wool yarn in warm water until the rinse has become completely clear. Shake the water from the yarn and hang it in the shade to dry.

Color: This recipe makes various shades of purple. The dye bath may be used again to obtain shades of lavender. It is fast.

Alternate fibers: Silk fibers dye well. Linen and cotton fibers do not dye well.

98. LOGWOOD WITH ALUM MORDANT

The dye is made from logwood chips and these can be purchased from commercial suppliers of vegetable dyestuffs. The chips come from a tropical tree which grows in Central America and the West Indies. A variety of colors can be made by using different mordants and different natural fibers.

Ingredients:

1 pound wool yarn, previously mordanted with alum
½ pound logwood chips
4 tablespoons tartaric acid
½ cup Glauber's salts

To make dye bath: Put the logwood chips in a cheesecloth bag, place the bag in an enamel container, cover it with two and a half gallons of warm water and soak for twelve hours. The chips should be packed loosely in the bag. After the bag has been allowed to soak, simmer it in the same water for one hour. Cool. Remove the bag. The liquid is now the dye bath.

To dye wool yarn: Add the wet, alum mordanted, wool yarn to the dye bath and simmer for thirty minutes. Dissolve four tablespoons of tartaric acid and half a cup of Glauber's salts in one pint of hot water and add this mixture to the dye bath. Simmer another fifteen minutes. Cool. Rinse the wool yarn in warm water until the rinse is clear, then squeeze the water from the yarn, and hang it in the shade to dry.

Color: This recipe makes a dark purple color. It is fast.

Alternate fibers: The recipe is a good one for all natural fibers. Vegetable fibers dye well.

99. MULBERRIES WITH ALUM MORDANT

Mulberries should be picked for dye purposes when they are ripe. They do not make a particularly good dye, but they can be used as a last resort.

Ingredients:

1 pound wool yarn, previously mordanted with alum
4 gallons ripe mulberries
4 tablespoons tartaric acid
½ cup Glauber's salts

To make dye bath: Place the mulberries in a five gallon enamel container, cover them with three and a half gallons of water and boil for about forty-five minutes. Crush the berries while they are boiling to remove as much color as possible. Cool. Strain. The liquid is the dye bath.

To dye wool yarn: Add the wet, alum mordanted, wool yarn to the dye bath; simmer for thirty minutes. Dissolve four tablespoons of tartaric acid and half a cup of Glauber's salts in one pint of hot water and add this mixture to the dye bath. Simmer another thirty minutes. Cool the wool yarn in the dye bath, then rinse it in warm water until the rinse is clear. Shake the water from the yarn, and hang it in the shade to dry.

Color: This recipe makes a gray-lavender; it is not a desirable color. One use of the dye bath exhausts the color.

Alternate fibers: No other fibers were tested.

100. WILD GRAPES WITH ALUM MORDANT

Wild grapes will only make a dye when they are ripe. When they are ripe they make a dark bluish-purple color. They can still be used for a few weeks after the frost has hit them.

Ingredients:

1 pound of wool yarn, previously mordanted with alum
4 gallons of wild grapes
4 tablespoons tartaric acid
½ cup Glauber's salts

To make dye bath: Pick the grapes from the stems, place them in a five gallon enamel container, cover them with water and boil for about an hour. The grapes should be crushed while they are boiling to release all of the coloring matter. Cool. Remove the refuse. The liquid is now the dye bath.

To dye wool yarn: Add the wet, alum mordanted, wool yarn to the dye bath and simmer for thirty minutes. Dissolve four tablespoons of tartaric acid and half a cup of Glauber's salts in one pint of hot water and add this mixture to the dye bath. Simmer for another thirty minutes. Cool. Rinse the yarn in warm water until the rinse is clear. Squeeze the water from the yarn and hang it in the shade to dry.

Color: This recipe makes various shades of lavender. The color will fade if it is exposed to sunlight for long periods of time.

Alternate fibers: Silk fibers dye well but they will fade if exposed to sunlight. Linen and cotton fibers do not dye well.

IX. Tans and Browns

There are an abundant number of dye materials for tans and browns; many grow wild and others can be purchased commercially. Some materials will dye only as dark as tan. However, this color can also be obtained by diluting a brown dye with water. Browns are top dyed with blue to make black.

101. ACORNS WITH ALUM MORDANT

The acorns should be collected after they are mature. They can be picked from the tree or off the ground. Last season's supply should not be picked from the ground because the color has been bleached from them by the weather.

Ingredients:

1 pound wool yarn, previously mordanted with alum
3 gallons acorns nuts and hulls
4 tablespoons tartaric acid
½ cup Glauber's salts

To make dye bath: Place the acorns in a five gallon enamel container, cover them with about three and a half gallons of water and soak for twelve to twenty-four hours. After they have been allowed to soak, boil the acorns in the same water for two hours. Cool. Remove the refuse. The liquid is the dye bath.

To dye wool yarn: Add the wet, alum mordanted, wool yarn to the dye bath and simmer for thirty minutes. Dissolve four tablespoons of tartaric acid and half a cup of Glauber's salts in one pint of hot water and add this to the dye bath. Simmer another thirty minutes. Cool the yarn in the dye bath. Rinse in warm water until the rinse has become completely clear. Shake the water from the yarn and hang it in the shade to dry.

Color: This recipe makes shades of tan and the color is fast.

Alternate fibers: Silk fibers dye about the same as wool. The color is too light for vegetable fibers.

102. ALKANET ROOTS WITH ALUM MORDANT

Alkanet roots can be purchased from commercial suppliers and the variety of the plant, as well as the mordant, determines the color.

Ingredients:

1 pound wool yarn, previously mordanted with alum
½ pound dried alkanet roots
4 tablespoons tartaric acid
½ cup Glauber's salts

To make dye bath: Place the dried alkanet roots in an enamel container, cover with two and a half gallons of warm water and soak for twelve hours. After they have been allowed to soak, boil the roots in the same water for about two hours. Cool. Remove the refuse. The liquid is now the dye bath.

To dye wool yarn: Add the wet, alum mordanted, wool yarn to the dye bath and simmer for thirty minutes. Dissolve four tablespoons of tartaric acid and half a cup of Glauber's salts in one pint of hot water and add this to the dye bath. Simmer another thirty minutes. Cool. Rinse the yarn in warm water until the rinse is clear. Shake or squeeze the water from the yarn and hang it in the shade to dry.

Color: This recipe makes shades of tan that have a reddish tone. It is fast.

Alternate fibers: All other natural fibers dye but the color will be very light.

103. BARBERRY PLANT WITH ALUM MORDANT

The green and red leaf varieties of the barberry plant make good dyes with little difference in the colors which result. The plant should be cut in late summer and fall. It may be used fresh or dry. The dry plant gives a lighter color.

Ingredients:

1 pound wool yarn, previously mordanted with alum
4 gallons cut up pieces barberry plant
4 tablespoons tartaric acid
½ cup Glauber's salts

To make dye bath: Cut the barberry canes and leaves into 3" or 4" lengths, and bruise or crush the canes to help release the color. Place them in a five gallon enamel container, cover with three and a half gallons of water and soak for twenty-four hours. Boil the plant in the soaking water for three hours. Enough water should be added to keep materials covered if it boils away. Cool. Remove the refuse. The liquid is now the dye bath.

To dye wool yarn: Add the wet, alum mordanted, wool yarn to the dye bath; simmer for thirty minutes. Dissolve four tablespoons of tartaric acid and half a cup of Glauber's salts in one pint of hot water and add to the dye bath. Simmer another thirty minutes. Allow the yarn to cool in the dye bath. Rinse the yarn in warm water until the rinse is clear. Shake water from the yarn and hang it in shade to dry.

Color: This recipe makes a range of tan colors and is very fast.

Alternate fibers: The recipe is suitable for all natural fibers, including jute, sisal, raffia, and other grasses. Mohair dyes very well.

104. BEETS WITH ALUM MORDANT

Beets do not make the quality or color of dye that they appear to make. They can be used as a last resort, but they are not recommended as a good dye substance.

Ingredients:

1 pound wool yarn, previously mordanted with alum
10 pounds beets
4 tablespoons tartaric acid
½ cup Glauber's salts

To make dye bath: Wash the soil from the beets, place them in a five gallon enamel container, cover with about three and a half gallons of water and cook until the beets are soft. The beets may be used for food and the liquid becomes the dye bath.

To dye wool yarn: Add the wet, alum mordanted, wool yarn to the dye bath and simmer for about thirty minutes. Dissolve four tablespoons of tartaric acid and half a cup of Glauber's salts in one pint of hot water and add this to the dye bath. Simmer another thirty minutes. Cool. Rinse the yarn in warm water until the rinse is clear. Shake the water from the yarn and hang it in the shade to dry.

Color: This recipe makes various shades of tan and is fast.

Alternate fibers: Silk fibers dye about the same as wool. Vegetable fibers do not dye dark enough to be considered a color.

105. BLACKBERRY VINES WITH ALUM MORDANT

The vines and leaves of young blackberry plants produce stronger dyes than old plants. One and two year old plants will make good dyes. A good seasonal time for making dye from blackberry vines is about the middle of the summer, after the plants have had several weeks of hot sunshine. The cultivated or wild varieties may be used.

Ingredients:

1 pound of wool yarn, previously mordanted with alum
4 gallons young blackberry vines and leaves
4 tablespoons tartaric acid
½ cup Glauber's salts

To make dye bath: Cut the young blackberry vines and leaves into 1" to 3" lengths and fill a five gallon enamel container nearly full with them. Cover them with water and let them soak for about twelve hours. Boil for three to four hours. Cool. Remove the vines and leaves and the liquid becomes the dye bath.

To dye wool yarn: Add the wet, alum mordanted, wool yarn to the dye bath, heat slowly to simmer and hold there for thirty minutes. Add half a cup of Glauber's salts and four tablespoons of tartaric acid which has been previously dissolved in one pint of hot water. Mix it well into the liquid and simmer for another thirty minutes. Cool. Rinse the yarn in the warm water until rinse is clear. Squeeze the rinse from the yarn and hang it in the shade to dry.

Color: This recipe makes a reddish-tan and it is very fast.

Alternate fibers: Silk dyes well and to about the same shade as wool. Linen and cotton fibers are not receptive to this dye.

106. BLACK WALNUT HULLS WITH ALUM MORDANT

Black walnut hulls produce their best dye when they are used fresh and when the hulls are green and spotted with brown. However, they can be dried and used later. Do not make dye from walnuts that have been on the ground for a season.

Ingredients:

1 pound wool yarn, previously mordanted with alum
4 gallons black walnut hulls
4 tablespoons tartaric acid
½ cup Glauber's salts

To make dye bath: Break the hulls from the walnuts, place them in a five gallon enamel container, cover with water and allow them to soak for about twenty-four hours. At the end of twenty-four hours, add enough water to nearly fill the container. The water will be absorbed while the hulls are soaking. Boil for about three hours. Additional water may be needed to keep the hulls covered with liquid while they are boiling. Cool. Remove the solid matter. The liquid is now the dye bath.

To dye wool yarn: Add the wet, alum mordanted, wool yarn to the dye bath; simmer for about thirty minutes. Dissolve four tablespoons of tartaric acid and half a cup of Glauber's salts in one pint of hot water and add to the dye bath. Simmer another thirty minutes. Cool. Rinse the yarn in warm water until the rinse is clear. Shake the water from the yarn and hang it in the shade to dry.

Color: This recipe makes brown and the color is fast. The brown may become darker with age.

Alternate fibers: Silk dyes well. Linen and cotton do not dye brown and there are better methods for obtaining tan. Mohair dyes a rich dark brown. Raffia dyes well.

107. BLOODROOT AND CUDBEAR WITH ALUM MORDANT

This dye is made by combining equal parts of approximately equal strength dye liquids made from bloodroot and cudbear.

Ingredients:

1 pound wool yarn, previously mordanted with alum
4 ounces dried bloodroots
1 ounce cudbear
4 tablespoons tartaric acid
½ cup Glauber's salts

To make first half of dye bath: Soak four ounces of dried bloodroots in one and a half gallons of warm water for twelve hours. Simmer the roots in the water in which they have soaked for about one hour. Cool. Remove the roots. This is one half of the dye bath.

To make second half of dye bath: Dissolve one ounce of cudbear in one gallon of warm water. Combine the two liquids. This is the entire dye bath.

To dye wool yarn: Add the wet, alum mordanted, wool yarn to the dye bath and simmer for thirty minutes. Dissolve four ounces of tartaric acid and half a cup of Glauber's salts in one pint of hot water and add this to the dye bath. Simmer another thirty minutes. Cool. Rinse the yarn in warm water until the rinse is clear, then squeeze or shake the water from the yarn, and hang it in the shade to dry.

Color: This recipe makes shades of rich tan and the color is fast.

Alternate fibers: The recipe is not suitable for linen. Other natural fibers dye lighter shades of color than wool.

108. BURLEY TOBACCO WITH ALUM MORDANT

Green burley tobacco leaves were used to make this dye bath. The cured tobacco, its stalks, and some of the commercially packaged natural leaf chewing tobaccos may give other good results. The green tobacco should be used in late summer.

Ingredients:

1 pound wool yarn, previously mordanted with alum
2 pounds green burley tobacco leaves
4 tablespoons tartaric acid
½ cup Glauber's salts

To make dye bath: Cut the tobacco leaves into 4" to 6" length pieces, place them in a five gallon enamel container, cover with two and a half to three gallons of water and boil for about one hour. Cool. Remove the refuse. The liquid becomes the dye bath.

To dye wool yarn: Add the wet, alum mordanted, wool yarn to the dye bath and simmer for thirty minutes. Dissolve four tablespoons of tartaric acid and half a cup of Glauber's salts in one pint of hot water and add this to the dye bath. Simmer another thirty minutes. Cool the yarn in the dye bath. Rinse in warm water until the rinse is clear. Shake the water from the yarn and hang it in the shade to dry.

Color: This recipe makes shades of tobacco brown and is fast.

Alternate fibers: The recipe is suitable for all fibers.

109. COCKLEBUR WITH CHROME MORDANT

Cockleburs should be picked in late summer and can be used fresh or dried.

Ingredients:

1 pound wool yarn, previously mordanted with chrome
4 gallons cockleburs
4 tablespoons tartaric acid
½ cup Glauber's salts

To make dye bath: Cut the cockleburs from the stalks, place them in a five gallon enamel container, cover with water and soak for about twelve hours. If dried cockleburs are used, they should be soaked twenty-four hours. Boil the cockleburs in the water in which they have been allowed to soak for about two hours. Extra water should be added if needed. Cool. Remove the refuse. The liquid is now the dye bath.

To dye wool yarn: Add the wet, chrome mordanted, wool yarn to the dye bath; simmer for thirty minutes. Dissolve four tablespoons of tartaric acid and half a cup of Glauber's salts in one pint of hot water and add to the dye bath.

Color: This recipe makes shades of rich brown. It is a fast color. The dye bath may be used again for lighter shades.

Alternate fibers: Silk fibers dye well. Vegetable fibers dye well but the shade will be lighter than that produced in animal fibers.

110. COFFEE WITH ALUM MORDANT

The grounds from any of the percolator grinds of coffee will make dye after they have been used for making coffee beverage. The coffee bean and other forms of coffee may make dye, but they were not tested in these experiments.

Ingredients:

1 pound cotton yarn, previously mordanted with alum
3 one pound coffee cans packed tightly with coffee grounds
4 tablespoons tartaric acid
½ cup Glauber's salts
2 tablespoons tannic acid

To make dye bath: Place the coffee grounds in a lightweight cotton bag. The bag should be large enough to allow the grounds to move around inside it. Tie the top of the bag and place it in a five gallon enamel container. Cover with three gallons of warm water and boil for one hour. Remove the bag of coffee grounds. Add two tablespoons of tannic acid to the liquid. This is the dye bath.

To dye cotton yarn: Add the wet, alum mordanted, cotton yarn to the dye bath and boil for thirty minutes. Dissolve four tablespoons of tartaric acid and half a cup Glauber's salts in one pint of hot water and add this to the dye bath. Boil another thirty minutes. Cool. Rinse the yarn in warm water until the rinse is clear. Remove the water from the yarn and hang it in the shade to dry.

Color: This recipe makes a coffee color, and it is fast.

Alternate fibers: Soft linen fibers dye well. Wool and silk fibers also dye well and it is not necessary to use tannic acid in the dye.

111. DRIED POKEWEED BERRIES WITH ALUM MORDANT

Dried pokeweed berries can be used to make a dye. The berries can be dried by the dyer or they can be purchased from suppliers of vegetable dyes.

Ingredients:

1 pound wool yarn, previously mordanted with alum
2 pounds dried pokeweed berries
4 tablespoons tartaric acid
½ cup Glauber's salts

To make dye bath: Place two pounds of dried pokeweed berries in a five gallon enamel container, cover them with about three and a half gallons of water and allow to soak twelve hours. After twelve hours, boil the dried berries in the water in which they have been allowed to soak for one hour. Cool. Strain. The liquid becomes the dye bath.

To dye wool yarn: Add the wet, alum mordanted, wool yarn to the dye bath and simmer for thirty minutes. Dissolve four tablespoons of tartaric acid and half a cup of Glauber's salts in one pint of hot water and add this to the dye bath. Simmer another thirty minutes. Cool. Rinse the yarn in warm water until the rinse is clear. Shake the water out of the yarn and hang it in the shade to dry.

Color: This recipe makes various shades of brown and is fairly fast.

Alternate fibers: Silk dyes well. Linen and cotton fibers do not dye well.

112. FLORIBUNDA ROSE WITH ALUM MORDANT

Rose plants can be used to make dyes. If the roses are trimmed in the fall, before frost, the trimmings will make a dye. It is not necessary to destroy the plant as the canes and leaves that are used to make the dye are used only after they have had a summer's sunshine. Cut and use fresh late in the season, before frost.

Ingredients:

1 pound wool yarn, previously mordanted with alum
4 gallons floribunda rose stems and leaves
4 tablespoons tartaric acid
½ cup Glauber's salts

To make dye bath: Cut four gallons of floribunda rose stems and leaves into 3" or 4" lengths, place them in a five gallon enamel container, cover with water and soak for twelve hours. Boil the stems and leaves in the water in which they have been allowed to soak for about two hours. Add extra water as it boils away. Cool. Remove the refuse. The liquid is now the dye bath.

To dye wool yarn: Add the wet, alum mordanted, wool yarn to the dye bath and simmer for thirty minutes. Dissolve four tablespoons of tartaric acid and half a cup of Glauber's salts in one pint of hot water and add this to the dye bath. Simmer another thirty minutes. Cool the yarn in the dye bath, then rinse it in warm water until the rinse is clear. Shake the water from yarn and hang it in the shade to dry.

Color: This recipe makes various shades of tan and the colors are fast.

Alternate fibers: This recipe is suitable for all natural fibers. Vegetable fibers should be boiled in the dye bath but animal fibers should only be simmered.

113. GUM CATECHU WITH ALUM MORDANT

Gum catechu is also known as cutch. It will make a variety of colors when different mordants are used with it.

Ingredients:

1 pound wool yarn, previously mordanted with alum
½ pound gum catechu
4 tablespoons tartaric acid
½ cup Glauber's salts

To make dye bath: Place the gum catechu in an enamel container and add two and a half gallons of very warm water. Stir the liquid with your hands until the gum catechu has dissolved. The resin like substance becomes sticky and gummy when water is added and it must be stirred and mixed for about thirty minutes before it dissolves. This is the dye bath.

To dye wool yarn: Add the wet, alum mordanted, wool yarn to the dye bath and simmer for thirty minutes. Dissolve four tablespoons of tartaric acid and half a cup of Glauber's salts in one pint of hot water and add this to the dye bath. Simmer another thirty minutes. Cool. Rinse the yarn in warm water until the rinse is clear. Squeeze the water from the yarn and hang it in the shade to dry.

Color: This recipe makes a color range of browns and the color is fast.

Alternate fibers: The recipe is suitable for all natural fibers but the shade of color will vary.

114. GUM CATECHU WITH COPPERAS MORDANT

Gum catechu is also known as cutch. It is one of the best natural dyes and can be purchased from commercial suppliers.

Ingredients:

1 pound wool yarn, previously mordanted with copperas
½ pound gum catechu
4 tablespoons tartaric acid
½ cup Glauber's salts

To make dye bath: Place the gum catechu in an enamel container and add two and a half gallons of very warm water. Stir the liquid with your hands until the gum catechu has dissolved. The resin like substance becomes sticky and gummy when the water is added and it must be stirred and mixed for about thirty minutes before it dissolves. This is the dye bath.

To dye wool yarn: Add the wet, copperas mordanted, wool yarn to the dye bath and simmer for thirty minutes. Dissolve four tablespoons of tartaric acid and half a cup of Glauber's salts in one pint of hot water and add this to the dye bath. Simmer another thirty minutes. Cool. Rinse the yarn in warm water until the rinse is clear. Squeeze or shake the water from the yarn and hang it in the shade to dry.

Color: This recipe makes shades of dark brown. The copperas mordant will make darker shades than alum mordant with this particular dyestuff. It is fast.

Alternate fibers: Other natural fibers dye lighter shades than wool.

115. HICKORY WITH ALUM MORDANT

Hickory twigs about finger size in diameter should be selected for dye purposes. The leaves can also be used to make dye. Hickory should be cut in late summer until frost and it can be used fresh or dry. Fresh materials make stronger dyes.

Ingredients:

1 pound wool yarn, previously mordanted with alum
4 gallons pieces of hickory twigs and leaves
4 tablespoons tartaric acid
½ cup Glauber's salts

To make dye bath: Cut the hickory twigs and leaves into 1" to 3" lengths. Place them in a five gallon enamel container, cover with water, and soak for twenty-four hours. Boil the twigs and leaves in the soaking water for about three hours. The water should be replenished as it boils away to keep the materials covered with water. Cool. Remove refuse. The liquid is now the dye bath.

To dye wool yarn: Add the wet, alum mordanted, wool yarn to the dye bath; simmer for thirty minutes. Dissolve four tablespoons of tartaric acid and half a cup of Glauber's salts in one pint of hot water and add this to the dye bath. Simmer another thirty minutes. Allow the yarn to cool in the dye bath. Rinse the yarn in warm water until the rinse is clear. Shake the water from the yarn and hang it in the shade to dry.

Color: This recipe makes various shades of tan and is fast.

Alternate fibers: This recipe is suitable for all natural fibers.

116. IRONWEED WITH ALUM MORDANT

To make a dye from ironweed, it should be cut when it is in bloom and used fresh. The entire plant, except the roots, may be used.

Ingredients:

1 pound wool yarn, previously mordanted with alum
4 gallons cut up pieces ironweed
4 tablespoons tartaric acid
½ cup Glauber's salts

To make dye bath: Cut the ironweed plant, blossoms, stems, and leaves into 3" to 4" lengths, cover with about three and a half gallons water and soak for about twelve hours. Boil the pieces of the plant in the water in which they have been allowed to soak for about two hours. More water may have to be added if it boils away. Cool. Remove the refuse. The liquid becomes the dye bath.

To dye wool yarn: Add the wet, alum mordanted, wool yarn to the dye bath; simmer for thirty minutes. Dissolve four tablespoons of tartaric acid and half a cup of Glauber's salts in one pint of hot water and add this to the dye bath. Simmer another thirty minutes. Allow the yarn to cool in the dye bath. Rinse the yarn in warm water until the rinse is clear. Shake the water from the yarn and hang it in the shade to dry.

Color: This recipe makes various shades of tan and the color is fast.

Alternate fibers: Silk fibers dye well. The color is too light for vegetable fibers.

117. LOGWOOD WITH NO MORDANT

This dye is made from logwood chips which can be purchased from commercial suppliers of vegetable dyestuffs. The trees grow in Central America and the West Indies. Many colors can be made with different mordants and different fibers.

Ingredients:

1 pound wool yarn
½ pound logwood chips
4 tablespoons tartaric acid
½ cup Glauber's salts

To make dye bath: Put the logwood chips in a cheesecloth bag, place the bag in an enamel container, cover it with two and a half gallons of warm water and soak for twelve hours. The chips should be packed loosely in the bag. After the bag has been allowed to soak, simmer it in the same water for one hour. Cool. Remove the bag. This is the dye bath.

To dye wool yarn: Add the wet, unmordanted, wool yarn to the dye bath and simmer for thirty minutes. Dissolve four tablespoons of tartaric acid and half a cup of Glauber's salts in one pint of hot water and add this to the dye bath. Simmer another thirty minutes. Cool. Rinse the yarn in warm water until the rinse is clear. Squeeze the water from the yarn and hang it in the shade to dry.

Color: This recipe makes a yellowish-red brown. It is fast.

Alternate fibers: The recipe is good for all natural fibers.

118. MADDER AND MULLEIN WITH CHROME MORDANT

This recipe combines dye baths. The dye baths are made separately then combined, in equal parts, to make one dye bath.

Ingredients:

1 pound wool yarn, previously mordanted with chrome
½ pound madder roots
2 gallons cut up pieces mullein
4 tablespoons tartaric acid
½ cup Glauber's salts

To make first half of dye bath: Cut the madder roots into ¼" to ½" lengths, place them in a three gallon enamel container, cover with two gallons of water and soak for twelve hours. The roots will expand and absorb some of the water. Simmer the roots in the water in which they have been allowed to soak for about forty-five minutes. Cool. Remove the roots. The liquid is the first half of the dye bath.

To make second half of dye bath: Cut the mullein stalks and leaves into 3" or 4" lengths, place them in a container, cover with two gallons of water and soak for twelve hours. After the stalks have been allowed to soak, boil them in the same water for three hours. Extra water may need to be added to keep materials covered. Cool. Remove refuse. This is second half of the dye bath. Combine equal parts of the two dye baths, one and a half gallons of each. The liquid is now ready for use as the dye bath.

To dye wool yarn: Add the wet, chrome mordanted, wool yarn to the dye bath; simmer for thirty minutes. Remember to keep the container covered when working with chrome. Dissolve four tablespoons of tartaric acid and half a cup of Glauber's salts in one pint of hot water and add to the dye bath. Simmer another fifteen minutes. Cool the yarn in dye bath, then rinse it in warm water until the rinse is clear. Shake the water from the yarn and hang it in the shade to dry.

Color: This recipe makes a brown color that has a red tone; it is an unusual shade. This is an extremely fast color.

Alternate fibers: Suitable for all natural fibers.

119. MULTIFLORA ROSE WITH ALUM MORDANT

The canes and leaf fronds of the multiflora rose can be used as a dye substance. They should be cut for dye purposes in late summer until frost.

Ingredients:

1 pound of wool yarn, previously mordanted with alum
4 gallons fresh, cut up, multiflora rose stems and leaves
4 tablespoons tartaric acid
½ cup Glauber's salts

To make dye bath: Cut the canes and leaves of the multiflora rose into 1" to 3" lengths. Place them in a five gallon enamel container, cover with water and soak for twenty-four hours. After they have been allowed to soak, boil the rose canes and stems in the same water for two hours. Extra water should be added if the water boils away. Cool the rose canes in the water. Remove the refuse. The liquid is now the dye bath.

To dye wool yarn: Add the wet, alum mordanted, wool yarn to the dye bath and simmer for thirty minutes. Dissolve four tablespoons of tartaric acid and half a cup of Glauber's salts in one pint of hot water and add this to the dye bath. Simmer another thirty minutes. Cool. Rinse the yarn in warm water until the rinse is clear. Shake the water from the yarn and hang it in the shade to dry.

Color: This recipe makes shades of tan and the color is fast.

Alternate fibers: Silk fibers dye well. Linen and cotton fibers dye lighter shades of color than wool and silk. Vegetable fibers dye very well if some metal is spun with the fibers.

120. PECAN HULLS WITH CHROME MORDANT

The green hulls from mature pecans make the best dye. Pecans can be picked off the ground or from the tree in late summer; the mature nut has a green hull with brown spots on it. The whole fruit can be used if it is crushed and soaked. Green pecan leaves and twigs will also make dye. Dried pecan materials make much lighter dyes than fresh ones.

Ingredients:

1 pound wool yarn, previously mordanted with chrome
2 gallons crushed pecan hulls
4 tablespoons tartaric acid
½ cup Glauber's salts

To make dye bath: Crush the pecan hulls, the nut and shell may be left inside the hulls, place them in a five gallon enamel container, cover with three gallons of water and soak for twelve to twenty-four hours. After the hulls have been allowed to soak, boil them in the same water for about two hours. Cool. Remove the refuse. The liquid is now the dye bath.

To dye wool yarn: Add the wet, chrome mordanted, wool yarn to the dye bath and simmer for thirty minutes. Dissolve four tablespoons of tartaric acid and half a cup of Glauber's salts in one pint of hot water and add this to the dye bath. Simmer another thirty minutes. Cool the yarn in the dye bath. Rinse the yarn in warm water until the rinse is clear. Shake the water from the yarn and hang it in the shade to dry.

Color: This recipe makes shades of rich dark golden brown and the color is fast.

Alternate fibers: This recipe is suitable for all fibers. Jute dyes exceptionally well.

121. PRIVET WITH ALUM MORDANT

The clippings from a privet hedge can be used to make a dye if they are cut from midsummer to frost. Fresh clippings should be used.

Ingredients:

1 pound wool yarn, previously mordanted with alum
4 gallons cut up privet clippings
4 tablespoons tartaric acid
½ cup Glauber's salts

To make dye bath: Cut the pieces of privet into 1" to 3" lengths, place them in a five gallon enamel container, cover with three gallons of warm water and soak for twelve hours. Boil the cuttings in the soaking water for about two hours. Cool. Remove the refuse and the liquid becomes the dye bath.

To dye wool yarn: Add the wet, alum mordanted, wool yarn to the dye bath and simmer for thirty minutes. Dissolve four tablespoons of tartaric acid and half a cup of Glauber's salts in one pint of hot water and add to the dye bath. Simmer another thirty minutes. Cool. Rinse the yarn in warm water until the rinse is clear. Squeeze the water from the yarn and hang it in the shade to dry.

Color: This recipe makes a color range of tans and light browns. It is fast.

Alternate fibers: This recipe can be used with any natural fiber.

122. QUEEN ANNE'S LACE WITH CHROME MORDANT

Queen Anne's lace is also known as wild carrot. This plant should be gathered when it is in bloom and the stems, leaves, and blossoms used for dye materials. They should be used fresh.

Ingredients:

1 pound silk yarn, previously mordanted with chrome
4 gallons cut up pieces Queen Anne's lace
4 tablespoons tartaric acid
½ cup Glauber's salts

To make dye bath: Cut the whole plant, including the blossoms, into 3" or 4" lengths, place them in a five gallon enamel container, cover with water and boil for about two hours. Extra water should be added if it boils away. Cool. Remove refuse. The liquid is the dye bath.

To dye silk yarn: Add the wet, chrome mordanted, silk yarn to the dye bath; simmer for thirty minutes. Remember to keep the container covered when working with chrome. Dissolve four tablespoons of tartaric acid and half a cup of Glauber's salts in one pint of hot water and add this to the dye bath. Simmer another thirty minutes. Allow the yarn to cool in the dye bath, then rinse it in warm water until rinse has become completely clear. Shake the water from the yarn and hang it in the shade to dry.

Color: This recipe makes colors which range from tan to light brown. The colors are fast.

Alternate fibers: The recipe is suitable for all natural fibers.

123. RED CEDAR WITH CHROME MORDANT

The red cedar is known as juniper in some geographical areas. The berries and twigs were collected in late August for this recipe. However, other seasons may give different colors.

Ingredients:

1 pound wool yarn, previously mordanted with chrome
4 gallons red cedar berries and twigs
4 tablespoons tartaric acid
½ cup Glauber's salts

To make dye bath: Cut the twigs with berries on them into 4" to 6" length pieces, place them in a five gallon enamel container, cover with about three and a half gallons of water and soak for twenty-four hours. After they have been allowed to soak, boil the twigs and berries in the same water for two hours. Cool. Remove the refuse. The liquid is now the dye bath.

To dye wool yarn: Add the wet, chrome mordanted, wool yarn to the warm dye bath and simmer for thirty minutes. Dissolve four tablespoons of tartaric acid and half a cup of Glauber's salts in one pint of hot water and add this to the dye bath. Simmer another thirty minutes. Cool the yarn in the dye bath, then rinse it in warm water until the rinse is clear. Shake the water from the yarn and hang it in the shade to dry.

Color: The recipe makes various shades of red-brown and the color is fast.

Alternate fibers: This recipe is good for silk yarns. Vegetable fibers will dye lighter shades than animal fibers.

The dye gives the yarns a strong cedar odor which may make them moth-proof.

124. RED ONION SKINS WITH TIN MORDANT

Fibers, as well as mordants and natural conditions, will affect the color that is obtained in natural dyeing. Red onion skins are a good example of this—they produce a brown color range on vegetable fibers and a gold range on animal fibers. The dyer will find that each dye batch will be a slightly different shade, regardless of the type of fiber.

Ingredients:

1 pound cotton chenille or
    soft spun cotton yarn, previously mordanted with tin
4 gallons red onion skins
4 tablespoons tartaric acid
½ cup Glauber's salts

To make dye bath: Place four gallons of dry red onion skins in a five gallon enamel container, cover them with water and boil until the skins are almost clear. Cool. Remove the cooked skins. The liquid is now the dye bath.

To dye cotton chenille yarn: Add the wet, alum mordanted, chenille yarn to dye bath and boil for thirty minutes. Dissolve four tablespoons of tartaric acid and half a cup of Glauber's salts in one pint of hot water and add this to the dye bath. Boil another thirty minutes. (All vegetable fibers should be boiled in the dye bath.) Allow the yarn to cool in the dye bath, then rinse it in warm water until rinse has become completely clear. Squeeze out the water from the yarn and hang it in the shade to dry.

Color: This recipe makes colors which range from tan to brown and the colors are reasonably fast.

Alternate fibers: If red onion skins are used with tin mordant, the dye is suitable for all natural fibers. The color will vary with the fiber.

125. SAFFLOWER WITH ALUM MORDANT

Safflower powder can be purchased from commercial natural dye suppliers. The powder is made from the dried blossoms of the plant and it makes a good dye.

Ingredients:

1 pound wool yarn, previously mordanted with alum
1 pound safflower powder
4 tablespoons tartaric acid
½ cup Glauber's salts

To make dye bath: Place the safflower powder in a lightweight cotton bag, about 12" square in size, tie the top and place it in a five gallon enamel container. Cover with three and a half gallons of warm water and soak until all of the powder is wet. Boil for about two hours and then remove the bag of powder. The liquid is the dye bath.

To dye wool yarn: Add the wet, alum mordanted, wool yarn to the dye bath and simmer for thirty minutes. Dissolve four tablespoons of tartaric acid and half a cup of Glauber's salts in one pint of hot water and add to the dye bath. Simmer another thirty minutes. Cool. Rinse the yarn in warm water until the rinse is clear. Shake water from the yarn and hang it in the shade to dry.

Color: This recipe makes shades of yellowish-tan and the color is fast. The dye bath may be used more than once to obtain lighter shades of color.

Alternate fibers: Silk fibers dye well. Linen and cotton fibers dye lighter shades than silk and wool.

126. SASSAFRAS WITH ALUM MORDANT

Sassafras twigs and leaves can be used to make a dye if they are cut in late summer until frost.

Ingredients:

1 pound wool yarn, previously mordanted with alum
4 gallons sassafras twigs and leaves
4 tablespoons tartaric acid
½ cup Glauber's salts

To make dye bath: Cut the sassafras twigs and leaves into 1" to 3" lengths. Place them in a five gallon enamel container, cover with water and soak for twenty-four hours. After they have been allowed to soak, boil the twigs and leaves in the same water for about three hours. More water may need to be added if it boils away. Cool. Remove the refuse. The liquid becomes the dye bath.

To dye wool yarn: Add the wet, alum mordanted, wool yarn to the dye bath and simmer for thirty minutes. Dissolve four tablespoons of tartaric acid and half a cup of Glauber's salts in one pint of hot water and add this to the dye bath. Simmer for another thirty minutes. Cool. Rinse the yarn in warm water until the rinse is clear, then shake the water from the yarn and hang it in the shade to dry.

Color: This recipe makes various shades of tan, which often have a reddish tone. The dyed yarn retains the color very well.

Alternate fibers: Silk fibers dye well. Linen and cotton dye a shade that is too light to be considered a color.

127. SCARLET SAGE BLOSSOMS WITH COPPERAS MORDANT

This plant is also known as salvia. The blossoms should be picked when they are in full bloom and they can be used fresh or dry. If the blossoms are exposed to extended hot sunshine it will make the pigment stronger and these blossoms give the best dye.

Ingredients:

1 pound soft spun linen yarn
4 ounces copperas crystals (ferrous sulfate)
4 gallons scarlet sage blossoms
4 tablespoons tartaric acid
½ cup Glauber's salts

To make dye bath: Pick the blossoms from their stems and place them in a five gallon enamel container, cover with water, and boil for about thirty minutes. Cool. Remove the blossoms. Add four ounces copperas crystals (ferrous sulfate) to the dye bath and stir them until the copperas has completely dissolved. This is the dye bath.

To dye linen yarn: Add the wet linen yarn to the dye bath and boil for thirty minutes. Dissolve four tablespoons of tartaric acid and half a cup of Glauber's salts in one pint of hot water and add this to the dye bath. The yarn should be kept covered with the dye bath to prevent streaking. Boil another thirty minutes. Cool the yarn in the dye bath, then rinse it in warm water until the rinse is clear. Wring the water from the yarn and hang it in the shade to dry.

Color: The recipe makes colors which range from tan to brown. It is fast.

Alternate fibers: This recipe may be used on cotton, but it is not suitable for animal fibers.

128. SEAWEED WITH ALUM MORDANT

The seaweed for this dye was collected from the coast of Maine. The color of the dye obtained from seaweed often varies according to the geographical area of its origin and the variety of the plant used to make the dye. Seaweed has a pungent odor when it is heated.

Ingredients:

1 pound of silk yarn, previously mordanted with alum
4 gallons of seaweed
4 tablespoons tartaric acid
½ cup Glauber's salts

To make dye bath: Pack the seaweed in a five gallon enamel container, cover it with water and boil for about two hours. Additional water should be added as the water in the container boils away, and putting a lid on the container helps to reduce the odor while the seaweed is boiling. Cool. Remove the solid matter. The liquid becomes the dye bath.

To dye silk yarn: Add the wet, alum mordanted, silk yarn to the dye bath and simmer for about thirty minutes. Dissolve four tablespoons of tartaric acid and half a cup of Glauber's salts in one pint of hot water and add this to the dye bath. Simmer another thirty minutes. Cool. Rinse the yarn in warm water until the rinse is clear. Squeeze the water from the yarn and hang it in the shade to dry.

Color: This recipe makes a light tan color which is fast.

Alternate fibers: Wool will dye gray when this recipe is used. The color is too light to be used on linen and cotton.

129. SEDGE WITH ALUM MORDANT

Sedge is a tall grass that grows in clumps in wet ground. It can be cut for dye purposes from spring until frost. The whole plant, except roots, yields dye substance.

Ingredients:

1 pound wool yarn, previously mordanted with alum
4 gallons cut up sedge
4 tablespoons tartaric acid
½ cup Glauber's salts

To make dye bath: Cut the sedge into 6" to 12" lengths, place them in a five gallon enamel container, cover with water, and boil for about two hours. The water may boil away and extra water should then be added. Cool. Remove the refuse. The liquid becomes the dye bath.

To dye wool yarn: Add the wet, alum mordanted, wool yarn to the dye bath and simmer for thirty minutes. Dissolve four tablespoons of tartaric acid and half a cup of Glauber's salts in one pint of hot water and add this to the dye bath. Simmer another thirty minutes. Cool. Rinse in warm water until the rinse is clear, then shake water from the yarn and hang it in the shade to dry.

Color: This recipe makes shades which range from greenish-tan to brass. It is one of the fastest of all the vegetable dyes.

Alternate fibers: Silk fibers dye well. Cotton and linen dye reasonably well but not as dark in color as wool and silk.

130. SUMAC BERRIES WITH ALUM MORDANT

The red sumac makes one of the fastest of vegetable dyes because it contains tannic acid. Its berries, twigs, and leaves can be used fresh or dried. The berries should be used only after they have turned dark red, not later than a few weeks after frost.

Last year's berries, if they have been left out in the weather, will have been bleached too much to make dye. Do not use the white berry because it is poisonous.

Ingredients:

1 pound wool yarn, previously mordanted with alum
4 gallons fresh or dried sumac berries
4 tablespoons tartaric acid
½ cup Glauber's salts

To make dye bath: Cut or break the berry heads into small pieces, place them in a five gallon enamel container, cover with about three and a half gallons of water and soak for about twenty-four hours. Extra water may need to be added to keep the berries covered. After the berries have been allowed to soak, boil them in the same water for two to three hours, depending on whether a dark or light color is desired. Cool. Remove the refuse. The liquid becomes the dye bath.

To dye wool yarn: In this case mordanting is not absolutely necessary but it is preferable because the fibers can be top dyed later. Add wet, alum mordanted, wool yarn to the dye bath and simmer for thirty minutes. Dissolve four tablespoons of tartaric acid and half a cup of Glauber's salts in one pint of hot water and add this to the dye bath. Simmer another thirty minutes. Cool. Rinse the yarn in warm water until rinse is clear, then shake water from yarn and hang it in the shade to dry.

Color: This recipe makes shades of tan and the color is very fast.

Alternate fibers: The recipe may be used with all natural fibers.

131. SUNFLOWER SEEDS WITH ALUM MORDANT

The mature dried sunflower seeds should be used.

Ingredients:

1 pound wool yarn, previously mordanted with alum
2 pounds dried sunflower seeds
4 tablespoons tartaric acid
½ cup Glauber's salts

To make dye bath: Place sunflower seeds in an enamel container, cover with three gallons of warm water and soak for twelve to twenty-four hours. After the seeds have been allowed to soak, boil them in the same water for two hours. Cool. Remove the seeds. The liquid becomes the dye bath.

To dye wool yarn: Add the wet, alum mordanted, wool yarn to the dye bath and simmer for thirty minutes. Dissolve four tablespoons of tartaric acid and half a cup of Glauber's salts in one pint of hot water and add this to the dye bath. Simmer another thirty minutes. Cool. Rinse the yarn in warm water until the rinse is clear. Shake the water from the yarn and hang it in the shade to dry.

Color: This recipe makes a yellowish-tan color and it is fast.

Alternate fibers: The color is too light to dye other fibers.

132. TEA WITH ALUM MORDANT

The black teas, sold for beverages, will make dyes and experiments can be made with the various commercial forms. Tea leaves can also be used for dye purposes after they have been used for making beverages. Allow two to three times the original amount when fresh dry leaves are not used.

Ingredients:

1 pound wool yarn, previously mordanted with alum
½ pound fresh dry black tea leaves
4 tablespoons tartaric acid
½ cup Glauber's salts

To make dye bath: Put the tea leaves in an enamel container. Pour two gallons of boiling water over the leaves and steep them for one hour. Strain. The liquid becomes the dye bath.

To dye wool yarn: Add the wet, alum mordanted, wool yarn to the dye bath and simmer for thirty minutes. Dissolve four tablespoons of tartaric acid and half a cup of Glauber's salts in one pint of hot water and add this to the dye bath. Simmer another thirty minutes. Cool. Rinse the yarn in warm water until the rinse is clear. Squeeze the water from the yarn and hang it in the shade to dry.

Color: This recipe makes shades of tan. It is fast.

Alternate fibers: The recipe can be used with all natural fibers.

133. TERRA-COTTA CLAY WITH ALUM MORDANT

The terra-cotta clay used by potters will make a dye. Experiments can also be made with other clays the dyer finds in his own area to see if they will make dyes.

Ingredients:

1 pound wool yarn, previously mordanted with alum
2 pounds dry terra-cotta clay
4 tablespoons tartaric acid
½ cup Glauber's salts

To make dye bath: Place the dry terra-cotta clay in a five gallon enamel container, add three and a half gallons of water and mix until the clay has dissolved. Boil the mixture and stir at the same time for about forty-five minutes. Cool. This is the dye bath.

To dye wool yarn: Add the wet, alum mordanted, wool yarn to the dye bath and simmer for thirty minutes. Move the dye bath around while it is simmering to keep the clay from settling to bottom of container. Dissolve four tablespoons of tartaric acid and half a cup of Glauber's salts in one pint of hot water and add this to the dye bath. Simmer another thirty minutes, keeping the yarn moving in the dye bath. Cool. Rinse the yarn in warm water until rinse is clear and make sure all the clay has been removed from the yarn. Shake the water from the yarn and hang it in the shade to dry.

Color: This recipe makes various shades of brown, and the color is fast.

Alternate fibers: Cotton fibers dye shades of brown. Silk and linen fibers were not tested.

134. TOMATO VINE WITH ALUM MORDANT

The tomato vine was used the next morning after frost. Fresh tomato vines may also be used for dyes.

Ingredients:

1 pound wool yarn, previously mordanted with alum
4 gallons cut up pieces of tomato vine
4 tablespoons tartaric acid
½ cup Glauber's salts

To make dye bath: Cut the tomato vine, leaves, and stalk into 3" or 4" lengths, about four gallons in quantity. Place them in an enamel container, cover with water and boil for about two hours. Extra water should be added if it boils away. Cool. Remove the refuse. The liquid is the dye bath.

To dye wool yarn: Add the wet, alum mordanted, wool yarn to the dye bath; simmer for thirty minutes. Dissolve four tablespoons of tartaric acid and half a cup of Glauber's salts in one pint of hot water and add this to the dye bath. Simmer another thirty minutes. Cool the yarn in the dye bath, then rinse it in warm water until the rinse is clear. Shake the water from the yarn and hang it in the shade to dry.

Color: This recipe makes shades of tan and the color is fast.

Alternate fibers: Silk fibers dye well. Vegetable fibers dye very pale.

135. TOMATO VINE WITH BLUE VITRIOL MORDANT

The green tomato vine was cut in August and used fresh. All of the plant parts above the ground were used. The variety of the tomato and the growing season will influence the shade of color.

Ingredients:

1 pound jute yarn, previously mordanted with blue vitriol
2 large tomato vines
4 tablespoons tartaric acid
½ cup Glauber's salts

To make dye bath: Cut the tomato vines into 4" to 6" length pieces. The two vines should make approximately four gallons of cut up pieces. Place them in a five gallon enamel container, cover with water, and boil for one and a half to two hours. Cool. Remove refuse. The liquid becomes the dye bath.

To dye jute yarn: Add the wet, blue vitriol mordanted, jute yarn to the dye bath and boil for thirty minutes. Dissolve four tablespoons of tartaric acid and half a cup of Glauber's salts in one pint of hot water and add this to the dye bath. Boil another thirty minutes. Cool the yarn in the dye bath, then rinse it in warm water until the rinse is clear. Wring the water from the yarn and hang it in the shade to dry.

Color: This recipe makes a range of tan colors that have green tones. The color is fast.

Alternate fibers: The recipe is suitable for all fibers.

136. TOMATO VINE WITH TIN MORDANT

The tomato vine was cut and used fresh in August. All of the green parts which were above the ground were used. The variety of the tomato and the growing conditions of the season influence the shade of color.

Ingredients:

1 pound wool yarn, scoured only
2 large tomato plants
4 tablespoons tartaric acid
½ cup Glauber's salts
1 teaspoon tin

To make dye bath: Cut the tomato plants into 4" to 6" length pieces. The two plants should make approximately four gallons of cut up pieces. Place in a five gallon enamel container, cover with three and a half to four gallons of water and boil for one and a half to two hours. Cool. Remove the refuse. Add one teaspoon of tin and mix well. This is the dye bath.

To dye wool yarn: Add the wet, scoured, wool yarn to the dye bath and simmer for thirty minutes. Dissolve four tablespoons of tartaric acid and half a cup of Glauber's salts in one pint of hot water and add this to the dye bath. Simmer another thirty minutes. Cool the yarn in the dye bath, then rinse it in warm water until the rinse is clear. Shake the water from the yarn and hang it in the shade to dry.

Color: This recipe makes a range of red-brown colors and is fast.

Alternate fibers: Silk fibers dye well. Vegetable fibers were not tested.

X. Grays and Blacks

There are comparatively few sources of black dye substances among the vegetable dye materials. About the only sources are some barks, a few of the varieties of wild roses, cochineal mixed with vinegar using a copperas mordant, and black walnut hulls. However, black can be made by top dyeing brown with blue.

Grays are easily obtained. Many plant parts make a dye as dark as gray and all of the black dyes can be diluted with water to make gray. After a black dye has been used once to produce black, it usually gives a gray the second and third times it is used. Vegetable fibers are much more difficult to dye black than animal fibers.

A small amount of black dye bath added to colors such as red and green will make them darker.

137. BARBERRY PLANT WITH COPPERAS MORDANT

The green and red leaf varieties of the barberry plant make good dyes and very little difference in color results. The plant should be cut in late summer and fall. It may be used fresh or dry. The dry plant gives a lighter color.

Ingredients:

1 pound jute yarn
4 ounces copperas crystals (ferrous sulfate)
4 gallons cut up pieces barberry plant
4 tablespoons tartaric acid
½ cup Glauber's salts

To make dye bath: Cut the barberry canes and leaves into 3" or 4" lengths and bruise or crush the canes to help release the color. Place them in a five gallon enamel container, cover with three and a half gallons of water and soak for twenty-four hours. After the barberry has been allowed to soak, boil it in the same water for three hours. Enough water should be added to keep the materials covered, if it boils away. Cool. Remove the refuse. Add four ounces of copperas crystals (ferrous sulfate) to the liquid and stir until completely dissolved. This is the dye bath.

To dye jute yarn: Add the wet, jute yarn to the dye bath; boil for thirty minutes. Dissolve four tablespoons of tartaric acid and half a cup of Glauber's salts in one pint of hot water and add this mixture to the dye bath. Boil another thirty minutes. Keep the yarn covered with the dye bath to prevent streaking. Allow the yarn to cool in the dye bath, then rinse the yarn in warm water until the rinse is clear. Wring the water from the yarn and hang it in the shade to dry.

Color: This recipe makes colors which range from gray to black. It is fast.

Alternate fibers: The recipe is suitable for all vegetable fibers.

138. BLACK WALNUT HULLS WITH COPPERAS MORDANT

Black walnut hulls will make a stronger dye if they are picked and used while the hulls still have some green coloring on the outside of the hull. After turning brown the hulls will still make a dye but it will not be as strong. The whole walnut may be dried and used later, although the results are variable. The walnuts should not be left lying on the ground for a season and then used for dye purposes. as they will

Ingredients:

1 pound wool yarn
4 ounces copperas crystals (ferrous sulfate)
4 gallons black walnut hulls
4 tablespoons tartaric acid
½ cup Glauber's salts

To make dye bath: Break the hulls from the walnuts, place them in a five gallon enamel container, cover with water and allow them to soak about twenty-four hours. At the end of this time add enough water to nearly fill the container. The water will be absorbed while the hulls are soaking. Boil for about three hours. Additional water may be needed to keep the hulls covered with liquid while they are boiling. Cool. Remove the solid matter. The liquid is now the dye bath. Add four ounces of copperas (ferrous sulfate) and stir until dissolved. The dye bath is ready to use.

To dye wool yarn: Add wet, wool yarn to the dye bath and simmer for about thirty minutes. Dissolve four tablespoons of tartaric acid and half a cup of Glauber's salts in one pint of hot water and add to the dye bath. Simmer another thirty minutes. Cool. Rinse in warm water until the rinse is clear. Shake the water from the yarn and hang it in the shade to dry.

Color: This recipe makes black and the color is fast. The dye bath may be used again to make shades of gray.

Alternate fibers: Copperas should not be used on silk fibers. Linen and cotton will dye various shades of gray.

139. BLACK WALNUTS AND INDIGO WITH ALUM MORDANT

A good black can be obtained by dyeing the yarn brown with black walnut hulls and then dyeing it a second time with indigo.

Ingredients:

1 pound wool yarn, previously mordanted with alum

3 gallons black walnut hulls
1 ounce indigo extract
4 tablespoons tartaric acid
½ cup Glauber's salts

To make first dye bath: Break the hulls from the walnuts, place them in a five gallon enamel container, cover with three gallons of warm water and soak for about twenty-four hours. After the walnuts have been allowed to soak, boil them in the same water for about three hours. Cool. Remove the refuse. The liquid is now the dye bath.

To dye wool yarn the first time: Add the wet, alum mordanted wool yarn to the dye bath and simmer for about one hour. Cool. Rinse the yarn in warm water until rinse is clear, then squeeze the water from the yarn, and hang it in the shade to dry.

To make second dye bath: Put two and a half gallons of warm water in an enamel container, add one ounce of strong indigo extract and mix well. This is the second dye bath.

To dye wool yarn the second time: Wet the walnut dyed yarn in warm water, add it to the second dye bath and simmer for fifteen minutes. Dissolve four tablespoons of tartaric acid and half a cup of Glauber's salts in one pint of hot water and add this mixture to the dye bath. Simmer another fifteen minutes. Cool. Rinse the yarn in warm water until the rinse is clear, then squeeze the water from the yarn, and hang it in the shade to dry.

Color: This recipe makes black and the color is fast.

Alternate fibers: Other natural fibers dye various shades of gray and these colors are fast.

140. COCHINEAL WITH COPPERAS MORDANT

Cochineal may be purchased in powder form from natural dye supply sources. When it is used with different mordants, shades of red, purple, and black may be obtained.

Ingredients:

1 pound of wool yarn
4 ounces copperas crystals (ferrous sulfate)
1 pound powdered cochineal
2 cups white vinegar
4 tablespoons tartaric acid
½ cup Glauber's salts

To make dye bath: Mix the cochineal powder with the white vinegar to form a paste. A one gallon glass or enamel container should be used for this because the mixture will expand and become very thick. Allow the mixture to stand for about twelve hours and stir it three or four times during this time. After this, transfer the mixture to a five gallon enamel container and add three gallons of warm water. The water should be added slowly and stirred at the same time to dissolve the lumps and thick masses of powder in the original mixture. Add four ounces of copperas crystals (ferrous sulfate) and mix until completely dissolved. Heat the liquid, simmer and hold there for about ten minutes. This is the dye bath.

To dye wool yarn: Add the wet yarn to the dye bath and simmer for thirty minutes. Dissolve four tablespoons of tartaric acid and half a cup of Glauber's salts in one pint of hot water and add this mixture to the dye bath. Simmer for another thirty minutes. Cool. Rinse the yarn in warm water until the rinse is clear. Shake the water out of the yarn and hang it in the shade to dry.

Color: This recipe makes black and the color is fast. The dye bath may be used again to obtain shades of gray. Each successive dyeing will produce a lighter shade.

Alternate fibers: Copperas should not be used on silk fibers. Linen and cotton will dye shades of gray. Jute dyes shades of dark gray.

141. ELDERBERRIES WITH TIN MORDANT

The purple-black variety of elderberries is used for this recipe. The berries may be used fresh or frozen, but in either case they should be used before they ferment. Berries that are absolutely ripe will make the strongest dye.

Ingredients:

1 pound wool yarn, previously mordanted with tin
4 gallons elderberries
4 tablespoons tartaric acid
½ cup Glauber's salts

To make dye bath: Cut the elderberries and the part of the stem nearest the berry into 1" to 3" lengths. Place them in a five gallon enamel container, cover with water and boil for about one hour. The berries should be crushed while they are boiling and more water can be added if needed. Cool. Strain. The liquid is the dye bath.

To dye wool yarn: Add the wet, tin mordanted, wool yarn to the dye bath; simmer it for thirty minutes. Dissolve four tablespoons of tartaric acid and half a cup of Glauber's salts in one pint of hot water and add this mixture to the dye bath. Simmer another thirty minutes. Cool the yarn in the dye bath, then rinse it in warm water until the rinse is clear. Shake the water from the yarn and hang it in the shade to dry.

Color: This recipe makes a dark blue-gray and the color is reasonably fast. The dye bath may be used again to produce lighter shades.

Alternate fibers: Silk fibers dye well. Vegetable fibers dye lighter shades than animal fibers.

142. ELDERBERRIES AND POKEWEED BERRIES WITH CHROME MORDANT

This recipe combines dye baths. The baths are made separately, then combined into one dye bath.

Ingredients:

1 pound wool yarn, previously mordanted with chrome
2 gallons elderberries
2 gallons pokeweed berries
4 tablespoons tartaric acid
½ cup Glauber's salts

To make first half of dye bath: Cut elderberries and the stem nearest the berry into 1" to 3" lengths. Place them in a container, cover with water, and boil for about one hour. Cool. Strain. This is one half of the dye bath.

To make second half of dye bath: Cut pokeweed berries and the stem nearest the berry into 1" to 3" lengths. Place them in a container, cover with water, and boil for about forty-five minutes. Cool. Strain. This is the second half of the dye bath. Pour the two liquids into a five gallon enamel container and stir. This is the completed dye bath, consisting of equal parts of the two dye liquids.

To dye wool yarn: Add the wet, chrome mordanted, wool yarn to the dye bath; simmer for thirty minutes. Remember, keep the container covered when working with chrome. Dissolve four tablespoons of tartaric acid and half a cup of Glauber's salts in one pint of hot water and add to the dye bath. Simmer another thirty minutes. Cool. Rinse the wool yarn in warm water until rinse is clear, then shake the water from the yarn and hang it in the shade to dry.

Color: This recipe makes various shades of green-gray which have a brown tone. When two dye liquids are combined they often produce unusual shades of color which are difficult to describe. It is fast.

Alternate fibers: Silk fibers dye well. Vegetable fibers dye lighter shades than animal fibers.

143. GUM CATECHU WITH COPPERAS MORDANT

Gum catechu is also known as cutch. It is a good dye and makes a variety of colors when different mordants are used with it. It can be purchased from commercial suppliers.

Ingredients:

1 pound wool yarn
4 ounces copperas crystals (ferrous sulfate)
½ pound gum catechu
4 tablespoons tartaric acid
½ cup Glauber's salts

To make dye bath: Place the gum catechu in an enamel container and add two and a half gallons of very warm water. Stir the liquid with your hands until the gum catechu has dissolved. The resin-like substance becomes sticky and gummy when water is added, and it must be stirred and mixed for about thirty minutes before it dissolves. Add four ounces of copperas and mix well. Heat to simmer and hold there for five minutes. This is the dye bath.

To dye wool yarn: Add the wet, scoured, wool yarn to the dye bath and simmer for thirty minutes. The yarn should be kept entirely covered with the dye bath to prevent streaking. Dissolve four tablespoons of tartaric acid and half a cup of Glauber's salts in one pint of hot water and add this mixture to the dye bath. Simmer another thirty minutes. Cool. Rinse the wool yarn in warm water until the ' rinse is clear. Squeeze or shake water from the yarn and hang it in the shade to dry.

Color: This recipe makes black and the color is fast.

Alternate fibers: Natural fibers, other than wool, dye various shades of gray.

144. LOGWOOD WITH CHROME MORDANT

The dye is made from logwood chips which can be purchased from commercial suppliers of vegetable dyestuffs. The chips come from a tropical tree native to Central America and the West Indies. A variety of colors can be made from this dye by using it with different mordants and different natural fibers.

Ingredients:

1 pound wool yarn, previously mordanted with chrome
½ pound logwood chips
4 tablespoons tartaric acid
½ cup Glauber's salts

To make dye bath: Put the logwood chips in a cheesecloth bag, place the bag in an enamel container, cover with two and a half gallons of warm water and soak it for twelve hours. The chips should be packed loosely in the bag. After the bag has been allowed to soak, simmer it in the same water for one hour. Cool. Remove the bag. The liquid becomes the dye bath.

To dye wool yarn: Add the wet, chrome mordanted, wool yarn to the dye bath and simmer for thirty minutes. Dissolve four tablespoons of tartaric acid and half a cup of Glauber's salts in one pint of hot water and add this mixture to the dye bath. Simmer another thirty minutes. Cool. Rinse the wool yarn in warm water until the rinse is clear. Squeeze the water from the yarn and hang it in the shade to dry.

Color: The recipe makes black color on wool. It is fast.

Alternate fibers: This recipe produces different colors on different natural fibers. It makes dark blue on silk.

145. MULTIFLORA ROSE WITH COPPERAS MORDANT

The canes and leaf fronds of the multiflora rose yield a dye substance. They should be cut for dye purposes between late summer and frost.

Ingredients:

1 pound wool yarn
4 ounces copperas crystals (ferrous sulfate)
4 gallons fresh cut up multiflora rose stems and leaves

4 tablespoons tartaric acid
½ cup Glauber's salts

To make dye bath: Cut the canes and leaves of the multiflora rose into 1" to 3" lengths. Place them in a five gallon enamel container, cover them with water and soak for twenty-four hours. After they have soaked, boil the canes and leaves in the same water for two hours. Extra water may be needed as it boils away. Cool. Remove the refuse. Add four ounces of copperas crystals (ferrous sulfate) to the liquid and stir the crystals into the liquid until they have completely dissolved. This is the dye bath.

To dye wool yarn: Add the wet, wool yarn to the dye bath and simmer for thirty minutes. Dissolve four tablespoons of tartaric acid and half a cup of Glauber's salts in one pint of hot water and add this mixture to the dye bath. Simmer another thirty minutes. Cool. Rinse the yarn in warm water until the rinse is clear. Shake the water from the yarn and hang in the shade to dry.

Color: This recipe produces colors which range from black to gray and is fast.

Alternate fibers: Copperas should not be used on silk fibers. Linen and cotton fibers dye shades of gray.

146. PECAN HULLS WITH COPPERAS MORDANT

The green hulls from mature pecans make the best dye. The pecans can be picked off the ground, or from the tree, in late summer. When it is picked, the nut should be mature; the hull is still green but it has brown spots on it. The whole fruit can be used if it is crushed and soaked. Green pecan leaves and twigs also make dye. Dried pecan materials will make lighter dyes than fresh ones.

Ingredients:

1 pound jute yarn
2 gallons crushed pecan hulls
2 ounces copperas
4 tablespoons tartaric acid
½ cup Glauber's salts

To make dye bath: Crush the pecan hulls, the nut and shell may be left inside the hulls, place them in a five gallon enamel container, cover with three gallons of water and soak for twelve to twenty-four hours. Boil the hulls in the water in which they have been allowed to soak for about two hours. Cool. Remove the refuse. Add two ounces of copperas to the liquid, and stir until dissolved. This is the dye bath.

To dye jute yarn: Add the wet, jute yarn to the dye bath and boil gently for about one hour. Dissolve four tablespoons of tartaric acid and half a cup of Glauber's salts in one pint of hot water and add this mixture to the dye bath. Boil gently for another thirty minutes. Cool the yarn in the dye bath. Rinse the yarn in warm water until the rinse is clear. Wring the water from the yarn, and hang it in the shade to dry.

Color: This recipe makes a color range of grays and blacks. It is fast. If jet black is desired, add four ounces of copperas instead of two.

Alternate fibers: The recipe is suitable for all fibers with the possible exception of silk. Wool fibers should be simmered in the dye bath for a total of one hour.

147. SASSAFRAS WITH COPPERAS MORDANT

Sassafras twigs and leaves make dyes if they are cut late in the summer and until frost. Mature leaves and twigs, about finger size in diameter, should be selected.

Ingredients:

1 pound wool yarn
4 ounces copperas crystals (ferrous sulfate)
4 gallons sassafras twigs and leaves cut up
4 tablespoons tartaric acid
½ cup Glauber's salts

To make dye bath: Cut the sassafras twigs and leaves into 1" to 3" lengths. Place them in a five gallon enamel container, cover with water, and soak for about twenty-four hours. After they have been allowed to soak, boil the twigs and leaves in the same water for about three hours. The water may need to be replenished if it boils away. Cool. Remove the refuse. Add four ounces copperas crystals (ferrous sulfate) to the liquid, and stir until completely dissolved. This is the dye bath.

To dye wool yarn: Add the wet, wool yarn to the dye bath and simmer for thirty minutes. Keep the yarn covered with the dye bath while the liquid is simmering to prevent streaking. Dissolve four tablespoons of tartaric acid and half a cup of Glauber's salts in one pint of hot water and add this to the dye bath. Simmer another thirty minutes. Cool. Rinse in warm water until the rinse is clear, then shake the water from the yarn and hang it in the shade to dry.

Color: This recipe makes colors which range from dark gray to black. The dye bath may be used again to produce lighter shades of gray. The color is fast.

Alternate fibers: Cotton and linen fibers dye lighter shades of gray than wool. Copperas should not be used on silk fibers.

148. SEAWEED WITH ALUM MORDANT

The color obtained from seaweed may depend on the geographical location where it is collected and on the variety of the plant. Different fibers may also produce different colors.

Ingredients:

1 pound of wool yarn, previously mordanted with alum
4 gallons of seaweed
4 tablespoons tartaric acid
½ cup Glauber's salts

To make dye bath: Pack the seaweed in a five gallon enamel container, cover it with water and boil for about two hours. Additional water should be added as the water in the container boils away. Since seaweed has a pungent odor, putting a lid on the container will help to reduce the odor while it is boiling. Cool. Remove the solid matter. The liquid becomes the dye bath.

To dye wool yarn: Add the wet, alum mordanted, wool yarn to the dye bath and simmer for about thirty minutes. Dissolve four tablespoons of tartaric acid and half a cup of Glauber's salts in one pint of hot water and add this to the dye bath. Simmer another thirty minutes. Cool. Rinse the yarn in warm water until the rinse has become completely clear, squeeze or shake out the last rinse and hang the yarn in the shade to dry.

Color: This recipe makes a gray color and is fast.

Alternate fibers: The recipe will make a tan color when silk fibers are used. Linen and cotton dye to a shade that is too light to be considered a color.

149. SUMAC BERRIES WITH COPPERAS MORDANT

The berries, twigs, and leaves of the red sumac can be used to make a dye when fresh or dry. They should be used only after the berries have turned dark red and for a few weeks after frost. Last year's berries should not be used if they have been left out in the weather. The white berry variety of sumac should not be used because it is poisonous.

Ingredients:

1 pound wool yarn
4 ounces copperas crystals (ferrous sulfate)
4 gallons of broken heads of sumac berries
4 tablespoons tartaric acid
½ cup Glauber's salts

To make dye bath: Break the berry heads into small pieces, place them in a five gallon enamel container, cover with water, and soak for twenty-four hours. Boil the berry pieces in the water in which they have been allowed to soak for about three hours. Extra water may be needed if it boils away. Keep about three and a half gallons of water in the container. Cool. Remove refuse. Add four ounces of copperas crystals (ferrous sulfate) to the liquid and stir until it has completely dissolved. This is the dye bath.

To dye wool yarn: Add the wet wool yarn to the dye bath and simmer for thirty minutes. Dissolve four tablespoons of tartaric acid and half a cup of Glauber's salts in one pint of hot water and add to the dye bath. Simmer another thirty minutes. Cool. Keep the yarn covered with the dye bath at all times to prevent streaking. Rinse the yarn in warm water until rinse is clear. Shake the water from the yarn and hang it in the shade to dry.

Color: This recipe makes colors which range between gray and gray brown. It is very fast.

Alternate fibers: Copperas should not be used on silk fibers. This is a good dye for vegetable fibers, but they dye lighter shades of color than wool.

150. SUNFLOWER SEEDS WITH COPPERAS MORDANT

Any variety of dried sunflower seeds may be used for making dyes.

Ingredients:

1 pound jute yarn
2 ounces copperas crystals (ferrous sulfate)
2 pounds dried sunflower seeds
4 tablespoons tartaric acid
½ cup Glauber's salts

To make dye bath: Place the sunflower seeds in an enamel container, cover them with three gallons warm water and soak for twelve hours. After they have been allowed to soak, boil the seeds in the same water for two hours. Cool. Remove the seeds. Add two ounces of copperas and stir it in until it has completely dissolved. This is the dye bath.

To dye silk yarn: Add the wet, scoured, jute yarn to the dye bath and simmer for twenty minutes. Keep the yarn entirely covered with the dye bath and stir the liquid frequently. Dissolve four tablespoons of tartaric acid and half a cup of Glauber's salts in one pint of hot water and add this to the dye bath. Simmer another thirty minutes. Cool. Rinse the yarn in warm water until the rinse is clear. Squeeze the water from the yarn and hang it in the shade to dry.

Color: This recipe makes shades of gray which usually have blue tones. It is fast.

Alternate fibers: This recipe is good for wool and cotton. It produces weak colors on linen.

151. WOOD CHARCOAL WITH COPPERAS MORDANT

Powdered wood charcoal can be purchased from drug stores and one can make it oneself.

Ingredients:

1 pound cotton yarn
8 ounces powdered wood charcoal
4 ounces copperas crystals (ferrous sulfate)
4 tablespoons tartaric acid
½ cup Glauber's salts

To make dye bath: Put about three and a half gallons of warm water in a five gallon enamel container, stir in eight ounces of powdered wood charcoal, and let it soak about twelve hours. Stir often. The charcoal will eventually dissolve. Heat the liquid to boiling and add four ounces of copperas crystals (ferrous sulfate). Stir until completely dissolved. This is the dye bath.

To dye cotton yarn: Add the wet, cotton yarn to the dye bath; boil for about thirty minutes. Dissolve four tablespoons of tartaric acid and half a cup of Glauber's salts in one pint of hot water and add this to the dye bath. Boil another thirty minutes, keeping the yarn covered with the dye bath to prevent streaking. Cool the yarn in the dye bath. Rinse in warm water until rinse is clear and wring the water from the yarn. Hang it in the shade to dry.

Color: This recipe makes colors which range between gray and black. It is fast.

Alternate fibers: Linen fibers should be treated in the same way as cotton. This recipe is not suitable for animal fibers.

XI. Sources of Supply

Many dye substances can be found in local areas and some individuals may prefer to cultivate their own supply, if the climatic conditions are favorable. Some of the dye substances which are not native to this country, and the mordants, will have to be purchased.

Drug stores can often supply the necessary chemicals from their own merchandise or by special order. Grocery stores, hardware stores, fishing and farm equipment supply stores, and supermarkets can be sources of supply for unusual natural fibers, condiments, beverages, soaps, etc.

Yarns are easily obtained from weaving supply companies and department stores.

Glauber's salts are much less expensive when purchased in one hundred pound quantities, or more, and usually from the local distributor of large chemical companies. It is really too expensive, from the dyer's standpoint, to purchase them by the pound.

CHARLES F. BAILEY

Dye substances and related materials can be purchased from Charles F. Bailey, St. Aubyn, 13 Dutton Street, Bankstown, N.S.W. 2200, Australia.

Dyes: The following dyes are priced by the ounce and can be ordered in one ounce or more quantities:

Indigo
Ruby cochineal
Carmine cochineal
Madder
Weld
Walnut
Logwood

Wools: Wools and other natural fibers are also available from Charles F. Bailey:

Superfine merino AAA 80's
Superfine merino AAA 70's
Merino 64's
Merino 58's/60's XB
Merino 50's XB

Merino 46's XB
Border Leicester
Romney Marsh
Cheviot
Natural colored merino
XB wools (black, brown, fawn, gray)
Rare fine black merino

Mohair

Mohair AAV
Superfine kid mohair

Silks

Tussah (wild) silk
Cultured silk

Cotton

Australian strict middling
1.1/16 inch raw cotton

Mr. Bailey states: "The wool classing system used in Australia is the Yorkshire Skein method. Briefly, this means that from 100's quality wool, 100 hanks, each consisting of 560 yards of yarn, could be spun to weigh 1 lb. This is only possible with the finest merino." All postage is extra and postage for small packets (fastest service) is 6¢ for each two ounces or part thereof. Transit time is from four to six weeks. Parcel charges are also extra. Postage for 1 to 5 lbs. is $2.50; 5 to 9 lbs., $3.40. Transit time is from six to eight weeks. The Australian banks accept personal checks drawn on United States banks, provided that 25¢ exchange fee is added. Mr. Bailey will send samples of wools air mail upon receipt of $1.50. Please note that prices for all materials are subject to change without notice.

DOMINION HERB DISTRIBUTORS

Dye substances can also be purchased from Dominion Herb Distributors, Inc., 61 Saint Catherine Street West, Montreal 18, Quebec, Canada.

The following dyes are available and they are sold in half a pound, one pound, and five pound quantities.

Dyes:

Indigo roots
Madder roots
Cochineal
Alkanet roots
Logwood chips
Cudbear
Quercitron (oak) bark
Black walnut hulls

Black walnut leaves
Red sandalwood chips
Henna leaves
Turmeric (curcuma)
Safflowers
Gum catechu (cutch)
Butternut bark
Bloodroot
Pokeberries
Fustic chips
Annatto seeds
Marigold petals (calendula)
Peach tree leaves
Nutgalls
Brazilwood chips
Osage orange chips

Mordants: The following list of mordants are sold in one fourth, half, and one pound quantities:

Blue vitriol (copper sulfate)
Tannic acid
Tartaric acid
Potassium or sodium dichromate (bichromate of potash)
Sodium hydrosulfite
Tin (stannous chloride)
Oxalic acid
Lime (calcium oxide)
Alum (potassium aluminum sulfate)
Copperas (ferrous sulfate)
Potassium permanganate
Ammonium sulphate, purified
Lead sulphate

There is a postage charge of 35¢ per pound on all merchandise. Two to three weeks should be allowed for delivery. Money orders and personal checks are accepted for payment. Again, prices are subject to change without notice.

NATURE'S HERB COMPANY

Various dyes are sold by Nature's Herb Company, 281 Ellis Street, San Francisco, California 94102.

Indigo is sold by ounce quantities, and normally this company can supply the following dyes.

Dyes:

Madder roots
Logwood chips
Fustic chips

Cochineal
Sage
Juniper berries etc.

Prices are subject to change without notice and postage is extra.

SPECTRO-CHEM INC.

Packaged quantities of some natural dyes and chemicals can be obtained from Spectro-Chem Inc., 1354 Ellison Avenue, Louisville, Kentucky 40204.

The prices of the dyes vary with the current market and the company can be contacted for information on what dyes are available, at what price. Postage is included in the package price.

CRAFT AND HOBBY BOOK SERVICE

Out of print and foreign publications can often be obtained from the Craft and Hobby Book Service, Big Sur, California 93920.

XII. Color Information Chart

DYE SUBSTANCE	APPROPRIATE MORDANT	COLOR RANGE	SUITABLE FIBER	COLOR FASTNESS
Acorns	Alum	Tans	Wool, silk	Excellent
Alkanet roots	No mordant	Gray-blues	Wool	Good
	Acetic acid	Red-purple-browns	Wool	Good
	Alum	Red-tans	All natural fibers	Good to fair
Annatto	Alum	Oranges	Wool, silk	Fair
Annatto and red onion skins	Tin	Dark yellows	Wool, silk	Good to fair
Barberry plant	Alum	Tans	All natural fibers	Excellent
	Blue vitriol	Greens	All natural fibers	Excellent
	Copperas	Dark greens	Wool	Excellent
	Copperas	Blacks and grays	Jute	Excellent
Beets	Alum	Tans	Wool, silk	Good to fair
Blackberries	Alum	Brown-purples	Wool, silk	Fair
	Tin	Purples	All natural fibers	Fair
Blackberry vines	Alum	Red-tans	Wool, silk	Excellent
Black walnut hulls	Alum	Browns and tans	All natural fibers	Excellent
	Copperas	Blacks and grays	All natural fibers	Excellent
Black walnut hulls and indigo	Alum	Blacks	Wool	Excellent
Bloodroot	No mordant	Oranges	Wool, silk	Good
	Alum	Oranges and rusts	Wool, silk	Good
	Tin	Reds and pinks	Wool, silk	Good
Bloodroot and cudbear	Alum	Tans	All fibers except linen	Good
Burley tobacco	Alum	Browns	All natural fibers	Good
	Blue vitriol	Green-browns	Wool, silk	Good
Butterfly weed blossoms	Alum	Yellows	All natural fibers	Good
Chrysanthemum blossoms	Alum	Yellows	Wool, silk	Good
Chrysanthemum blossoms and marigold blossoms	Alum	Golds, brasses	Wool, silk, cotton	Good

DYE SUBSTANCE	APPROPRIATE MORDANT	COLOR RANGE	SUITABLE FIBER	COLOR FASTNESS
Cochineal	Alum	Purple-reds	All natural fibers	Good
	Chrome	Purple	Wool, silk	Good
	Copperas	Black	Wool	Good
	Tin	Bright reds and pinks	All natural fibers	Good
Cochineal and indigo	Alum	Purples	Wool	Good
Cochineal and madder	Alum	Brown-purples	All natural fibers	Good
Cockleburs	Alum	Brasses	Wool, silk, cotton	Excellent
	Chrome	Browns	All natural fibers	Excellent
	Copperas	Dark greens	Wool	Good
Coffee	Alum	Tans	All natural fibers	Good
Concord grapes	Alum	Lavenders and purples	All natural fibers	Fair
	Tin	Purples	All natural fibers except linen	Fair
Crab apples (ornamental)	Alum	Pinks	Wool	Fair to poor
Cudbear	Alum	Reds	All natural fibers	Excellent
	Tin	Purples	All natural fibers	Excellent
Dahlia blossoms	Alum	Yellows	Wool, silk	Good
Dandelion blossoms	Alum	Light yellows	Wool, silk, soft cotton	Good
	Tin	Light, bright yellows	Wool, silk	Good
Day lily blossoms	Alum	Yellows	Wool, silk	Good to fair
	Chrome	Golds and brasses	Wool, silk	Good to fair
	Chrome	Tans and browns	Cotton, linen	Good to fair
	Tin	Bright yellows	Wool, silk	Good to fair
Elderberries	Alum	Purples	Wool, silk	Good
	Chrome	Blues	Wool, silk	Good
	Tin	Blue-grays	Wool, silk	Good
Elderberries and pokeweed berries	Chrome	Green-grays	Wool, silk	Good
Floribunda rose plant	Alum	Tans	All natural fibers	Good
	Copperas	Dark greens and blacks	Wool, cotton	Good
Fustic	Alum	Bright yellows	All natural fibers except linen	Excellent
	Blue vitriol	Greens	All natural fibers	Good
	Chrome	Golds and brasses	All natural fibers	Good
Fustic and indigo	Alum	Greens	All natural fibers except linen	Good
Fustic and madder roots	Alum	Oranges and rusts	All natural fibers	Good

DYE SUBSTANCE	APPROPRIATE MORDANT	COLOR RANGE	SUITABLE FIBER	COLOR FASTNESS
Goldenrod blossoms	Alum	Yellows	Wool, silk	Good
	Chrome	Golds	Wool, silk	Good
	Copperas	Dark yellow-greens	Wool	Good
	Tin	Bright yellows and golds	Wool, silk	Good
Goldenrod blossoms and indigo	Alum	Greens	Wool, silk, cotton	Good
Goldenrod plant	Copperas	Dark greens, gray-greens	Wool, cotton, linen	Good to fair
Gum catechu (Cutch)	No mordant	Rusts	All natural fibers	Excellent
	Alum	Browns	All natural fibers	Excellent
	Blue vitriol	Kahki and olive greens	All natural fibers	Excellent
	Copperas	Dark browns	All natural fibers	Excellent
	Copperas	Grays and blacks	Some wools and vegetable fibers	Excellent
Gum catechu and madder	Alum	Bright red-browns	All natural fibers	Excellent
Henna	Tin	Rusts and red-browns	Wool, silk	Good
Hickory	Alum	Tans	All natural fibers	Good
Hollyhock blossoms	Chrome	Oranges and rusts	Wool, silk	Good
Indigo (Method No. 1)	Alum	Blues	All natural fibers except linen	Excellent
Indigo (Method No. 2)	Alum	Dull blues	Wool	Good
Indigo (Method No. 1)	Chrome	Greens	Wool, silk	Good
Indigo and turmeric	Alum	Greens	Wool	Good
Ironweed	Alum	Tans	Wool, silk	Good
Lavender, and rosemary extract	Alum	Pinks	Wool	Good
Lily of the valley	Alum	Yellow-greens	Wool, silk	Good
	Chrome	Golds and rusts	Wool, silk	Good
	Tin	Bright yellows and golds	Wool, silk	Good
Logwood	No mordant	Blues	Wool	Good to fair
	No mordant	Browns	Silk and vegetable fibers	Good
	Alum	Dark purples	All natural fibers	Good
	Chrome	Dark blues	Silk	Good
	Chrome	Black	Wool	Good
	Copperas	Dark blues, blacks and grays	Wool	Good

DYE SUBSTANCE	APPROPRIATE MORDANT	COLOR RANGE	SUITABLE FIBER	COLOR FASTNESS
Madder (powder form)	Alum	Reds	All natural fibers	Excellent
	Tin	Bright reds and pinks	All natural fibers	Excellent
Madder (roots)	Alum	Reds	All natural fibers	Excellent
	Chrome	Oranges and rusts	All natural fibers	Excellent
Madder and mullein	Chrome	Red-browns	All natural fibers	Excellent
Madder and sedge	Alum	Rusts	All natural fibers	Excellent
Madder and yellow onion skins	Alum	Oranges and rusts	All natural fibers	Excellent
Marigold blossoms	Alum	Yellows	Wool, silk	Good
Mulberries	Alum	Gray-lavender	Wool	Poor
Mullein	Alum	Yellows	All natural fibers	Excellent
	Chrome	Golds	All natural fibers	Excellent
	Tin	Bright yellows	All natural fibers	Excellent
Multiflora rose plant	Alum	Tans	All natural fibers	Excellent
	Copperas	Blacks and grays	Wool and vegetable fibers	Good
Peach leaves	Alum	Yellows	Wool, silk	Good
	Tin	Bright yellows	Wool, silk	Good
Pecan hulls	Chrome	Golden browns	All natural fibers	Good
	Copperas	Blacks and grays	Wool and vegetable fibers	Good
Pokeweed berries	Alum	Reds	Wool, silk	Good
	Alum	Pinks	Cotton, linen	Good
	Chrome	Rusts	Wool	Good
	Tin	Bright reds	All natural fibers	Good
Pokeweed berries and red onion skins	Alum	Rusts	Wool, silk	Good
Dried pokeweed berries	Alum	Browns and rusts	Wool, silk	Good
Privet	Alum	Tans	All natural fibers	Good
	Blue vitriol	Greens	Wool	Good
	Copperas	Dark greens	Wool	Good
Queen Anne's lace	Alum	Pale yellows	All natural fibers	Good
	Chrome	Tans	All natural fibers	Good
Red cedar	Chrome	Red-browns	Wool, silk	Good
Red onion skins	Chrome	Golds	Wool, silk	Good
	Chrome	Tans	Cotton, linen	Good to fair
	Tin	Red-tans and browns	All natural fibers	Good
Safflower	Alum	Yellows and tans	Wool, silk	Good
	Copperas	Brasses	Wool	Good
	Tin	Golds and rusts	Wool, silk	Good

DYE SUBSTANCE	APPROPRIATE MORDANT	COLOR RANGE	SUITABLE FIBER	COLOR FASTNESS
Sassafras	Alum	Red-tans	Wool, silk	Good
	Copperas	Blacks and grays	Wool and vegetable fibers	Good
Scarlet sage blossoms	Alum	Pinks	Wool, silk	Good to fair
	Copperas	Tans and browns	Wool, cotton, linen	Good
Seaweed	Alum	Tans	Wool, silk	Good
	Copperas	Dark yellow-greens	Wool	Good
	Copperas	Grays	Cotton, linen, and some wools	Good
Sedge	Alum	Yellow-green-tans	All natural fibers	Excellent
	Chrome	Golds	All natural fibers	Excellent
	Copperas	Gray-greens	Wool, cotton, linen	Excellent
Sumac	Alum	Tans	All natural fibers	Excellent
	Blue vitriol	Greens	All natural fibers	Excellent
	Copperas	Grays and gray-browns	All natural fibers	Excellent
Sunflower seeds	Alum	Yellow-tans	Wool	Good
	Blue vitriol	Greens	Wool	Good
	Blue vitriol	Grays	Silk	Good
	Copperas	Gray-blues	Wool, cotton	Good
Tea	Alum	Tans	All natural fibers	Good
Terra-cotta clay	Alum	Tans and red-browns	Wool, cotton	Good
Tomato vines	No mordant	Red-browns	Wool, silk	Good
	Alum	Tans	Wool, silk	Good
	Blue vitriol	Green-tans and browns	All natural fibers	Good
Turmeric	Alum	Yellows	All natural fibers	Good to fair
	Blue vitriol	Greens	Wool	Good to fair
	Chrome	Golds and brasses	All natural fibers	Good to fair
Wild grapes	Alum	Lavenders	Wool	Fair
Wood charcoal	Copperas	Grays	Cotton, linen	Good
Yellow onion skins	Alum	Yellows	Wool, silk	Good
Zinnia blossoms	Alum	Yellows	Wool, silk	Good

XIII. Dye Substance Information Chart

DYE SUBSTANCE	PART OF PLANT USED FOR DYE	TIME TO COLLECT PLANT PARTS	TO PRESERVE DYE SUBSTANCE
Acorns	The whole nut. (Leaves, twigs, and bark from some of the oak trees make dyes.)	Collect nuts in fall. Collect leaves in late summer and fall. Collect twigs in late summer and fall. Collect bark in spring.	Use fresh or dry. Store dried parts in dry place.
Alkanet	Roots	Purchase commercially.	Store in dry place.
Annatto	Seeds Powder	Purchase commercially.	Store in dry place.
Barberry	All parts of the plant which are above ground.	Late summer and fall.	Use fresh or dry. Store dried parts in dry place.
Beets	Part below ground.	When beet is mature.	Use fresh.
Blackberries	Fruit	When completely ripe.	Use fresh or freeze.
Blackberry vines	One to two year old vines.	Late summer until frost.	Use fresh.
Black walnut	Hulls, the entire nut, leaves, twigs, and bark make dye.	The fruit, leaves, and twigs are best when some green is mixed with brown in late summer and fall. Collect bark in spring.	Use fresh or dry. Store dried material in dry place.
Bloodroot	Roots	Dig roots in summer. Roots can also be purchased.	Use fresh or dry. Store in dry place.
Burley tobacco	Leaves and stalks.	Late summer.	Use fresh or dry. Store dried material in dry place.
Butterfly weed	Blossoms	When in full bloom.	Use fresh.
Chrysanthemum	Blossoms	When in full bloom.	Use fresh or dry. Dried blossoms should be stored in porous container, keep in dry place.
Cochineal	Commercial powder	Purchase.	Store in dry place.
Cockleburs	Burs	Late summer and early fall.	Use fresh.
Coffee	Beans, grounds, and powder.	Purchase.	The usual home storage is sufficient.
Concord grapes	Fruit	When completely ripe.	Use fresh.

DYE SUBSTANCE	PART OF PLANT USED FOR DYE	TIME TO COLLECT PLANT PARTS	TO PRESERVE DYE SUBSTANCE
Crab apples (ornamental)	Fruit	When completely ripe.	Use fresh.
Cudbear	Powder made from lichen.	Purchase.	Store powder in dry place.
Dahlia	Blossoms	When in full bloom.	Use fresh or dry. Store dried blossoms in dry place.
Dandelion	Blossoms	When in full bloom.	Use fresh.
Day lily	Blossoms Leaves	When blossoms are in full bloom. Collect leaves in summer and until frost.	Use fresh.
Elder	Fruit	When completely ripe.	Use fresh or freeze.
Floribunda rose	The canes and leaves.	From midsummer until frost.	Use fresh.
Fustic	Bark	Purchase.	Store in dry place.
Goldenrod	Blossoms Plant	When in full bloom. Summer until frost.	Use fresh. Use fresh.
Gum catechu (cutch)	A resin-like substance.	Purchase.	Store in dry place.
Henna	Powder Leaves	Purchase. Purchase.	Store in dry place. Store in dry place.
Hickory	Hulls from the nuts, leaves, twigs, and bark.	Collect hulls in early fall. Leaves and twigs in late summer. Bark in spring.	Use fresh or dry. Store dried materials in a dry place.
Hollyhock	Blossoms	When in full bloom.	Use fresh.
Indigo	Plant Powder made from the plant.	The plant can be grown in this country. Powder can be purchased.	Author does not know how to preserve plant. Store powder in dry place.
Ironweed	All parts of the plant which are above ground.	Late summer.	Use fresh.
Lavender, and rosemary extract	Commercial extract	Purchase.	Store in air tight bottle, keep away from light.
Lily of the valley	Leaves	Late spring until frost.	Use fresh.
Logwood	Bark	Purchase.	Store in dry place.
Madder	Roots Powder form	Purchase. Purchase.	Store in dry place. Store in dry place.
Marigold	Blossoms	When in full bloom.	Use fresh or dry. Store dried blossoms in porous container.
Mulberry	Fruit	When completely ripe.	Use fresh.
Mullein	Leaves and stalks.	Late summer and early fall.	Use fresh or dry. Store dried materials in dry place.
Multiflora rose	Leaves and canes.	Late summer and early fall.	Use fresh.

DYE SUBSTANCE	PART OF PLANT USED FOR DYE	TIME TO COLLECT PLANT PARTS	TO PRESERVE DYE SUBSTANCE
Peach	Leaves	Summer and early fall.	Use fresh.
Pecan	Hulls, the entire nut, leaves, twigs, and bark.	Collect nuts in early fall. Collect leaves and twigs in late summer. Bark in spring.	Use fresh or dry. Store dried materials in dry place.
Pokeweed	Berries	When completely ripe.	Use fresh or dry. Store dried materials in dry place.
Privet	Leaves and twigs.	Summer and fall, until frost.	Use fresh.
Queen Anne's lace	All parts of the plant which are above the ground.	Late summer and early fall.	Use fresh.
Red cedar	Twigs	Late summer until freezing weather.	Use fresh.
Red onion skins	Dry skins of the mature onion bulb.	When onions are mature.	Use dry skins. Store dry skins in dry place.
Safflower	Powder made from dried blossoms.	Purchase.	Store powder in dry place.
Sassafras	Leaves, twigs, and bark.	Collect leaves and twigs in late summer. Collect bark in spring.	Use leaves and twigs fresh. Bark can be dried. Store bark in dry place.
Scarlet sage	Blossoms	When in full bloom.	Use fresh.
Seaweed	Plant	Any time.	Use soon after collected.
Sedge	Grass	Spring until frost.	Use fresh or dry. Store dried grass in dry place.
Sumac	Berries, twigs, and leaves.	Collect berries when ripe and until freezing weather. Twigs and leaves in late summer until frost.	Use fresh or dry. Store dried materials in dry place.
Sunflower	The mature dried seeds.	When seeds are mature and dried. Can be grown. Can be purchased.	Store in dry place.
Tea	Leaves, tea bags and powdered tea.	Purchase.	The usual home storage is sufficient.
Terra-cotta clay	Clay used for ceramics. Found clays.	Purchase. Any time.	Store dry or wet. Any practical way.
Tomato	Vines	Late summer and early fall.	Use fresh.
Turmeric	The condiment. Powder made from the plant for dye.	Purchase. Purchase.	Home storage is sufficient. Store dye powder in dry place.
Wild grapes	Fruit	When completely ripe.	Use fresh.
Wood charcoal	Charcoal from burned wood. Charcoal can be purchased in chunk and powder forms.	Any time.	Store in dry place.

Yellow onion skins	Dry skins from the mature onion bulb. The mature bulb.	When onions are mature. When onions are mature.	Store dry skins and mature bulbs in dry place.
Zinnia	Blossoms	When in full bloom.	Use fresh or dry. Store dried blossoms in porous container in dry place.

Bibliography

Bailey, L.H. *The Standard Encyclopedia of Horticulture.* (second edition) 3 vols. New York: The Macmillan Company, 1928.

Bolton, Eileen M. *Lichens for Vegetable Dyeing.* Newton Center, Massachusetts: Charles T. Branford Company, 1960.

Colton, Mary-Russell Ferrell. *Hopi Dyes.* Flagstaff, Arizona: The Museum of Northern Arizona, 1965.

Conley, Emma. *Vegetable Dyeing.* Penland, North Carolina: Penland School of Handicrafts, Inc., n.d.

Dana, Mrs. William Starr. *How to Know the Wild Flowers.* (revised edition) New York: Dover Publications, Inc., 1963.

Davidson, Mary Frances. *The Dye Pot.* Middlesboro, Kentucky: Published by the author, 1950.

Furry, Margaret S. and Viemont, Bess M. *Home Dyeing with Natural Dyes.* Miscellaneous Publication No. 230, United States Department of Agriculture. Washington: Government Printing Office, 1934.

Holding, May. *Notes on Spinning and Dyeing Wool.* (fourth edition) London: Skilbeck Brothers Limited, 1949.

Kierstead, Sallie Pease. *Natural Dyes.* Boston: Bruce Humphries, Inc., 1950.

Leggett, William F. *Ancient and Medieval Dyes.* Brooklyn: Chemical Publishing Company, Inc., 1944.

Mairet, Ethel M. *Vegetable Dyes.* (eleventh edition) London: Faber and Faber, Ltd., 1952.

Schetky, Ethel Jane and Staff. (ed.) *Dye Plants and Dyeing.* Brooklyn: Brooklyn Botanic Garden, 1964.

Thurstan, Violette. *The Use of Vegetable Dyes.* (seventh edition) London: The Dryad Press, 1957.

Wyeth Laboratories. *The Sinister Garden.* New York: Wyeth Laboratories, Division of American Home Products Corporation, 1966.

Index

Gum catechu, blue vitriol
mordant on wool No. 2

Indigo with chrome
mordant on wool

Indigo and turmeric with
alum mordant on wool

Lily of the valley with
alum mordant on wool

Sedge with copperas
mordant on mohair

Sunflower seeds, blue
vitriol mordant on wool

Sunflower seeds, blue
vitriol mordant on silk

Alkanet roots and acetic
acid on wool

Blackberries with alum
mordant on silk

Blackberries with tin
mordant on cotton

Cochineal with chrome
mordant on wool

Cochineal, madder, alum
mordant on mohair

Cudbear with tin mordant
on wool

Elderberries with alum
mordant on wool

Logwood with alum
mordant on wool

Logwood with alum
mordant on cotton

Logwood with alum
mordant on silk

Wild grapes with alum
mordant on wool

Alkanet roots with alum
mordant on wool

Blackberry vines with
alum mordant on wool

Black walnut hulls with
alum mordant on wool

Black walnut hulls with
no mordant on raffia

Bloodroot and cudbear
alum mordant on wool

Cocklebur with chrome
mordant on wool